For Siobhan

The Sad Lady of Lislee is dedicated to Brittany, daughter
of Autism diary keeper @AutismJournal

CONTENTS

Published by Black Cormorant Books
Copyright © 2014 Paul Kestell 1st edition
All rights reserved.
ISBN: 13:978-1501018336
ISBN-10: 10:1501018337

ACKNOWLEDGMENTS

Cover Photograph Courtesy of Anchor Bar Courtmacsherry

THE WEST CORK RAILWAY

When Grandad had drink taken he would lash out at her but she was well able, and if she wasn't, a fella wouldn't notice such as the bitchin' she did back at him. She took to calling him a geriatric, saying he was past it and no good. He was in fine fettle too, tearing into her and calling her a harlot and a slut. And that was no way for a man to talk to his daughter, but that never stopped either of them, as the same could be said of her and that it was no way to talk to your father. As the man said, there was a pair of them in it. Auntie Bridie said it was because we all lived together in such a small house. She said it was because of what happened to our Nan; she was always saying that. She went on about Niamh blaming Grandad, and Grandad blaming Niamh. Bridie said the truth was that it was neither of their fault, and that Nan just upped and died like other folk, and it was her turn and her time. Bridie was no real comfort now, don't misunderstand me, a harder bitch God never put on Earth, but sometimes she talked sense. Well, a little anyhow. I think she enjoyed talking about Nan, as it reminded her of better times when they were growing up. At least that was what she said. In fairness to the old trout, she gave me money on my birthdays and when I made my communion and my confirmation. But she really played a blinder when she told me all of this stopped when I was twelve, so that on my last birthday was the final payment and she gave me five euro instead of the two euro fifty she had given me up till then. I could never figure out what the fifty cent was for, then she said it was for sweets and I was to save the rest. Of course I spent the rest on sweets too. But she didn't check on my savings box that was tucked away safe under my bed. When the fight was over Grandad invariably would go to his room and bang the door, whilst Niamh would just sit at the kitchen table with her head in her hands. I was so used to this by now that any comfort I could give her became futile, as it was all part of a ritual. This time I walked into the kitchen and Niamh pretended to cry, but I could see her peeping through the cracks in her fingers. I took a seat opposite her, deliberately scraping the floor with the chair. She allowed her head to rock like it was controlled by her silent sobbing. I was quiet for a few minutes but then finally I said, 'He has some neck, sayin' I look like Marty Burke.' Niamh ignored me whilst she thought; then she released her fingers from her face and eyes.

'You could look like worse, Billy; he is as handsome as he is wild.'

'Tis wild, alright. Do you think I look like him so?'

'A bit, but that is no harm, sure. He is good looking.'

'He is I suppose.'

'All the Burkes are handsome, Billy. Even old Mr Burke. It's the sallow skin from the sun and the sea.'

'Is that what it is? Is that why Grandad don't like them, because they are handsome then?'

'Nah. He don't care about that. I wish it was that. Nah, he thinks Marty Burke won't marry me on account of you, but, sure, Marty is dying to marry me. It is me that tells him to go and feck himself. He might feckin' throw himself off the Coolim Cliffs for all I care. You see, that's the truth of it, Billy, we are grand with him being out in Coolbawn. I don't want him here in the village with me. Imagine the trouble.'

'If I look like him, it means that he must be my father then.'

'It does not. Your father just looked like them, that's all. He wasn't a Burke.'

'Then who was he?'

'He was a man I met. We were good for a while.'

'Ah, come on now, Niamh. You must have been very good.'

'We were. Now make me some tea. Your grandfather has upset me no end this time, and the smell of drink off him would kill a horse. He goes out all day sitting at the bar, hail fella well met, then he comes home here, with what? Abuse, Billy, just feckin' abuse!'

'Old people are like that,' I said.

'Collie's Grandad had to go into a home because he was so troublesome. He was doing scary things like walking around the garden in his nude, and Collie said that he told the district nurse that she was a big fat ride and she had to run out of the house when he took his lad out!'

'Bejesus, is that what we have to look forward to, boy? He is a scourge as he is!'

'You see?' I said as I put the kettle on. She watched me, waiting, as I took two mugs down from the hooks. I allowed her the favourite red one, and I took the blue one with the chip on the side.

'Old people are cranky, Niamh, 'cause they live in the past. They are always thinkin' back to when they were young, so they get jealous of young people like they know their number is comin' up. Do you get me?'

'You're a head of sense for a boy!'

'You see, Niamh, I am doin' this project at school. Me and Collie are sharin' it. It's all about the West Cork Railway and about how they closed it down against the wishes of the people.'

'Oh, God, don't start your Grandad off about all of that. He will never shut up about it, about his cousins and his uncles and their grandfathers and what else. The man goes demented when it comes up, so say feckin' nothing to him, Billy, will yah, or we will have no peace.'

'I didn't know Grandad knew anythin' about the railway.' I handed Niamh her mug, and she smiled gratefully.

'That and every other issue in the world, save for what he should know, Billy, like the price of coal and groceries, and what it costs to keep him, save for the few lousy euros he gives me, and I swear to you, boy, he is holdin' back. Telling me they have cut his pension!'

'How does he know about the railway?' I sat back in my seat. The tea could have been hotter; I was a divil for putting too much milk in. But I drank a gulp of it, and it was sound enough.

'He helped out on the pier when he was young, and he helped load the beet on to the trains. He goes on about his relations havin' built the railway and about the last train and how closin' the railway killed commerce around here.'

'Ah, Niamh, I will have to interview him. Don't worry, I will leave it till a quiet day. It won't hassle you at all. I will do it when you are at work.'

'Do, boy, but be prepared to be bored to death. Did you do your homework anyway?'

'I did, but I have a bit more to do before I go to sleep.'

'Have yah?'

'Just a bit, but I was gonna do it in bed.'

'Alright, but turn off the lamp before you go to sleep. Don't be wastin' the electric.'

'No bother.'

I finished my tea and said goodnight to her. The tears had vanished, but she had sort of black spots beneath her eyes. As soon as I was gone I could hear her on the phone to her friend, Mary. Niamh did most of the talking, but every now and then she would go quiet for a full minute.

*

They closed the West Cork Railway on March 31, 1961. The reasons were very clear and convincing to me. The whole damn thing was losing money. According to my research it had accumulated losses of £56,000. That stark

7

fact, coupled with falling passenger numbers, led to the decision. It was to my surprise that I read that the actual vote to close the railway was swung by only one member on the CIE board. This after thousands of signatures had been collected in a petition. One man from Clonakilty tried to take an action in the high court, but he gave way when he was told that he would have to pay all the costs should he lose. I suppose the poor bugger hadn't got the money to take on the might of CIE and the government.

*

One afternoon I decided to call over to see Collie to discuss my findings. I set off down the steep steps. Sliding my hand along the handrail gave me extra speed; I abseiled down on to the path. I ran down the street by the holiday cottages and on down by the two-storey houses.
I slowed to examine the old railway station. It now served as a dwelling, and it was in excellent repair. I ran on till I reached the pier and a few men stood around idle, stooping over an upturned rowing boat. They were laughing heartily as I passed by. I increased my speed, inhaling the cold air. I imagined the train coming in all the way to the pier and the men loading it with beet. But then I remembered hearing that the train also brought passengers in the height of summer, swelling the main street, and the local businesses were bursting with activity. Collie lived in a cottage just passed Church Corner, and his mother let me in. I was out of breath and I barely got out, 'Hello, Mrs Collins.' She stared at me for a moment to make sure that I was alright. Satisfied, she headed back to the kitchen. She was a big woman, from the rear anyhow. Some people in the village didn't like her because her husband worked in the bank doing mortgages, and he wasn't always able to oblige everyone, but Mrs Collins was always fair to me. She used to give me and Collie slabs of marble cake when we were

doing our homework or even when we were just acting the maggot like.

'How is Niamh?' she would always ask before saying, 'and old Tom, isn't he looking great for his age.'

I could only give the stock answer to all.

'They are grand, sure.'

Collie was impressed with my research, mainly because he hadn't bothered to do any of his own. Collie was one of the brainiest boys in our class but he was fierce lazy, and they threw him off the hurling team. Not because he wasn't any good but because he was brilliant and he just didn't try. So the coach got sick of him and sent him home with a note for his father.

'Sure all was the same then in the '60s? They had no money to pay for anythin'?' he said as he turned on his laptop. It was new and much better than the desktop I shared with Niamh and occasionally Grandad, when he took one of his notions.

'I have to leave it in the kitchen at night. My mother is mad, but my dad didn't care, like, but she listens to all those oul wan programmes on the radio.'

'Can you get the Wikipedia up?'

'I can, hold it a sec.'

Collie looked over his shoulder and then he said, 'Ssh.'

Satisfied there was no sound, he clicked and there was this naked women lying on her back. She had enormous breasts, and then this man came into the shot.

He had a huge lad on him, and she grabbed it.

'Collie, I am making tea!' his mother shouted from the hall.

'Alright!' he shouted back, clicking the image off and taking a deep breath.

'There is loads more, Billy. He puts it into her and all!'

'Wow!'

9

'I will show yah the next time, when she is out at the shops. There is loads more!'

'Wow!' I said again, not fully understanding why I said it. We continued on with our legitimate research, but Collie wasn't all that interested. His mother came in with a tray. She gave us a cup of tea and a slice of marble cake and I awaited her comments, but she surprised me by changing the mantra.

'I saw old Tom over in Centra. Is he a bit shook?

'I dunno, Mrs Collins. I think he is fine.'

'There's a terrible dose doin' the rounds. We all had it; well, save for Collie, thank God. But both his sisters and me and Edward came down with it. He looked very shook. Maybe he has the dose. Here, Collie, put that on the plate. Don't be getting crumbs on my carpet.'

The marble cake was lovely, and the tea washed it down perfectly.

'I can't wait till summer,' Collie said.

'I hate March. It is nothin', is it? Not summer, not winter. I am going to go out to Coolbawn. That Julie Burke will be hangin' around the Blind Strand, and she is waitin for the Collie!'

'You wish,' I said, writing notes about the Regatta festival train excursions to Baltimore.

'I know, boy. She is always given me the eye on the school bus. It is a given.'

'In your dreams!' I said, putting my cup and plate back on the empty tray.

'You are only jealous, Billy, 'cause you can't go near her. She might be related to you.'

'Related? Ah, no, Collie. Niamh says I am not a Burke at all. That's only in old Tom's imagination. He has a thing about the Burkes and the land out in Coolbawn. He thinks it should be his. Niamh says he is all mixed up about it, like.'

10

'Mixed up? Sure, you are the head off of Marty Burke, boy!'

'Nah, Niamh says it was some other fella that she was good with for a while, but to be fair she said he looked like the Burkes. Do you know what I mean, like?'

'Nah. I think Niamh is spoofin' yah?'

'I suppose. It is farfetched. Alright, Collie, I am goin' now. Tell yer mother thanks for the tea.'

'I will, sure, and the next day we can watch the rest of yer one, hah?'

'Jesus, boy, I can't wait,' I said, and off I went running again.

*

Cork, Bandon and South Coast Railway (CB&SCR) was an Irish gauge (1,600 mm (5 ft. 3 in)) railway. It opened in 1849 as the Cork and Bandon Railway. Its name was changed to Cork Bandon and South Coast Railway in 1888 and became part of the Great Southern Railway in 1924. The CB&SCR served the south coast of County Cork between Cork and Bantry. It had a route length of 94 miles (151 km), all of it single track. [Wikipedia]

That was a lot of track, and I was studying the map of the railway. Then I read about Goggins tunnel in Ballinhassig. It was now the longest abandoned tunnel in Ireland, measuring 828 metres end to end. The map fascinated me. I dunno, ever since I was small I always loved maps. All the place names: Cork, Bandon, Clonakilty, Baltimore. I was dying to show Collie my research as I had stuck the map on the top right hand of the page, and then I pasted photographs of Goggins tunnel and the viaduct at Halfway just below it. He would be pleased with my work, as so far he had done nothing. And the whole project had to be handed in by Friday, which gave us under a week. But as luck would have it, he dropped by with a football. He wanted to go over to the green and play three and in, so I left the project notes on the table and the two of us bounced down the steps. Collie kicked the ball and it landed right smack in the middle of the pitch, which was grand, mind you, no longer than twenty yards with steel goalposts each end. Many a great match was played here, and sometimes fathers brought their sons here to kick ball while the mammies brought the small ones to the playground that was adjacent to it. On this day we had the whole pitch to ourselves, and Collie for once was in the humour for playing.

'I found loads more for our project, Collie. I spent the last hour pasting photos and writing. I think we will be fine.'

'Yer a grand lad, Billy. To be honest I have done nothin'. The mother is wreckin' my head about the laptop. She won't let me use it in the bedroom no more. She is making me use it at the kitchen table. Like, what the fuck?'

Collie went in goal first, and it was hard to get one past him. He was skinny and lanky, and if the mood took him he could have a stormer and you might never score against him.

'She must be suspicious or somethin'. Maybe some oul wan has freaked her out.'

'Yeah, like yer Aunt Bridie. Wasn't she talkin' to her at the bingo?'

'Was she?' I said.

'I didn't know Bridie played Bingo.'

'She is a wizard at it. The priest was going to ban her, she was winning so much.'

Collie caught my first three shots, and then he deflected my fourth with his left knee. A woman coming from the playground threw the ball back to us, much to the delight of her little daughter.

'She never says a word about it.'

'Don't she?' Collie said, throwing the ball out to me like a professional.

12

'She don't want to share with ye all.'

'Yeah, that's likely,' I said.

'Got yah!' I dummied to his right but I slotted it in on his left and he was none too pleased, as he kicked the ball out way beyond me. It landed in the goal at the opposite end.

'What did yah do that for?' I screamed at him.

'Make ya work, won't it?'

It did, and I raced back to him with the ball. I planted one over his head, and it was in the net before he could lift his hands.

'Ya ballox,' he cursed and lazily went to retrieve the ball. I ran to the bank at the side doing a fake celebration, which annoyed him even more, and he attempted to lash the ball out of his hands. He miskicked, and it just went ballooning into the air and landed a yard behind me.

'Hah, serves you right! I shouted, and he steadied himself for a hard shot, but I just stroked into the far corner of the net. He made a spectacular dive but he was miles too late, and I ran behind the goal with my hands in the air mocking him. This really pissed him off, and he ran out taking the ball. He juggled it aggressively and lashed the ball into the empty net.

'One,' he said.

'Nah, you have to wait till I am in, Collie!'

'Hurry up, so, I will bury ya anyhow!'

'You will!'

'Easy!'

I saved everything he threw at me for a good five minutes, and he was becoming more and more frustrated with his shots rattling the bar. He even missed with some as he tried to hit the ball too hard. He was becoming closer to the Gansey marker, and I saved his next shot with my fingertips and pushed it around the post. It took him ages to retrieve the ball as it ran all the way down the path and into the playground itself, and he had to go on his knees to prise it from underneath the kiddie's slide.

He wasn't too pleased when he came back. He had a right go at me. The ball hit me on the side of the head, but I still managed to keep it out.

'I am fed up!' Collie said, picking up the ball and sitting on the ground.

'You are havin' a right stormer. If I were there till next week I wouldn't score against ya. Do you think she will let me have the laptop back?'

He sat on the grass beside his Gansey, and I went over and sat beside him. He was pulling at the grass like his fingers were desperate for something to do. It looked like a good idea so I did it as well, and the two of us picked up the blades of grass and threw them aimlessly away. I could see the hard earth underneath, and then I suddenly realised that without the grass this whole landscape would be a desert and it would be useless for football.

'I dunno, Collie, women are funny like that. Niamh wouldn't let me, I know. She is alright, but she is fierce fussy about that kind of thing. Now, she don't mind what I watch on the telly. She doesn't throw me out during the Tudors or anythin'.'

'Did yah see the Tudors? Ah, man, they are at it all of the time. The king is a horny bastard, isn't he?'

'He is,' I said.

'All those royalty are like that. They have to produce a male heir, isn't that it, so they go mad for the ridin'.'

'Me mother didn't watch it because of all the ridin' but me father watched it all, and I sat there on the couch not a peep out of me. I think he forgot I was there, Billy. Me sittin' there with me legs crossed all the time. Wasn't yer one Anne Boleyn a cracker?'

'She was, Collie. Niamh loved it. She never said nothin' to me, so I just watched it away. Sure, it's only ridin',' I said, getting up.

I kicked the ball into the empty net just to see if Collie was still interested, but he wasn't. He was flaked out now, lying on his back. I was hoping he wouldn't get a cold because it was getting colder as the breeze whipped up off the tide. He put on his Gansey as his hot sweat was cooling down.

On the way back across the street Collie kicked the ball at our house, missing the sitting room window by six inches. The ball miraculously landed by the railing and lay still. I was going to feck him out of it, but I couldn't help laughing and he laughed as well.

I asked him did he want to come in and look over the project, but then Grandad came shuffling up the street and Collie shook his head. I threw the ball to him, and off he went with a big hello to Grandad as he passed him. All I could hear was Grandad's restrained reply, 'Hello, son.'

I went in and closed the front door like I had never seen him coming. I heard him fluster with his keys; then it seemed like an age before he got the front door open. He stopped in the hall, and I heard him take off his overcoat and hang it on the coat stand. Moving slowly, his steps were laboured, and when he appeared at the kitchen door he was surprised to see me.

'I saw yer friend walkin down the street. Young Collins. He is gettin' tall!'

'We call him a lank.'

'A lank. I like that. There used to be two brothers lived up the street. We called them Little Lank and Big Lank. They were both over six foot, but one was younger. It was our way of explainin' who we were talkin' about.'

'I like that, Grandad. Little Lank!'

'It worked anyhow. People knew who yer were on about. What's that ya have there?'

15

'Collie and me, we are doin' a project at school on the West Cork Railway. I am puttin' it all together.'

'The West Cork Railway?'

'Yeah. Dah yah want tea?'

'Love one, son. Just what the doctor ordered, hey. I have a bit of a chest. It's a bugger.'

I put the kettle on, leaving my project open on the kitchen table. I knew Grandad was looking at it, even though I wasn't looking at him.

'My grandfather worked on the viaduct at Halfway, and his brothers worked on the railway all their lives. It was a livin' and the saddest day ever when they closed it.' He said.

'It was losin' money.' I said

'Losin' money?' Grandad raised his voice.

'But sure, it made more money, it was unreal. The people comin' out here on a Sunday and to Clonakilty and Baltimore, and the beet train and activity it gave. The money was huge, boy, huge!'

'I read its losses were up to £56,000.'

'It is paper money, Billy, what I call creative accountancy. These feckers wanted rid of it, because it was the fashion. They were closin' lines in the south of England then as well. What Mr Accountant did was a hatchet job. Why?'

'I dunno, Grandad.'

'Think about it? Think!'

I poured him his tea, and I even gave him my mug. He sat with my project book spread out in front of him.

'Because he didn't factor in two things: the value of the service, number one, and the future needs of the populace, number two. You see, Billy, the railway brought great business to the towns and villages it served, and the money made couldn't be counted. He wasn't thinkin' of the future either. Imagine if we still had the railway now. The population was growin'. I tell ya, we will have a railway again someday. It is only a matter of when.'

16

Grandad stopped talking to drink his tea, and in fairness I could see he was reading through my project from top to bottom.

'But the teacher says that businesses have to make profits, or they die.'

Grandad thought about what I said, and I was sure I had flummoxed him when he diverted and said, 'What time is yer mother home? Is she late this evenin'?'

'She is late, Grandad. It's Wednesday. She left us a stew in the fridge.'

'A stew. Alright, sure, we can heat it up, can't we?'

'I will do it if you want to watch the news.'

'You see, Billy,' he said, 'it is like this. There is private business, and there is state business. State business don't have to be profitable all on its own. It just has to be good for the citizen. Take the trains. They were losin' money right, but they were makin' money for other citizens and providin' a service. So the citizen thinks this is good and worth it. So as long as the citizen can make his profit overall, he can carry it. See what I am gettin' at? So it is all good, like.'

'Dunno, Grandad, I don't think the teacher would agree, what with the state of the country, like, and the debt and all. Doesn't everything have to make a profit to make sense?'

'What they did made no sense, Billy. Ya tell the teacher I said that, and he is makin' no sense either.'

'She.'

'Tell her yer Grandad sees no sense in her argument, because go her way and nothin' happens, like. Commerce and social good just stop. All business has a cost, Billy. Like, ya buy a bicycle from me for fifty euro then sell it on for a hundred. If you didn't have the cost, ya wouldn't see the profit. But this accountant just didn't want the cost, did he?'

'But he wasn't makin' the money, Grandad, was he? Other people were makin' it on the back of him. Isn't that what was wrong with him? Why should he do all just for others to make the dough, hah?'

'Because it wasn't his at all, Billy, it belonged to the people. The whole idea was that it served the public. Don't ya see?'

'Ah, Grandad, yer too smart for me. I didn't know ya had it in yah. This is not what our teacher says. Niamh says yer mad about the railway anyhow. Still can't see the sense. If a thing is not makin' dough, yah have to shut it down.'

'Never mind Niamh,' he said, bringing his mug over to the sink.

'Does she think that I don't read or listen or that I grew up here with my eyes closed? She wasn't born yet when the last train pulled out of here. She didn't know what it was like before they turned this village into a ghost town. Things were never the same again, boy. The whole region was affected, and it never recovered.'

Grandad coughed and for a minute I thought he was going to choke, but he cleared his throat with a grizzly sound.

'I am going inside to watch the news, but I tell ya, Billy, if you really want to know about the trains go see the captain down in Holland's. He is there most days. Go in after school, have a Coke. He will probably put one up for ya. He knows all about the trains. Nothin' he doesn't know.'

My Grandad made his way to the hall, and I watched the back of his head all grey fuzz leading to bald. He was kind of hunched over like he was carrying a weight, and I had never seen him hunch like that. Then I thought that he was probably playing up; but, then again, maybe he wasn't, such was the passion that had stuck to his words. In the end he had allowed a defeated acceptance grip him, and I noticed that his thin watery eyes were moist as he spoke.

18

I heated the stew for seven o' clock, and when I went in to call him he was asleep in the armchair with the television blaring and nobody watching. I had to call him twice to rise him, and it took him an age to get to his feet and follow me to the kitchen. I had done a fair job of heating the stew, even if it were burning hot on top and only tepid underneath, and it had a faint burned smell that was dark and musty, and it sort of came and went. I ate up all of mine, and Grandad ate his in silence.

*

'We are waiting for you, Collie. What sort of progress have you made? I would ask you, Billy, but I see you are bursting to tell me, so I thought I might ask your esteemed colleague here. So when did the West Cork Railway close, Mr Collins? Ssh, boys, come on now, I want these projects in by Friday, remember?' Collie looked blankly at Miss Forde. She in turn looked up to the ceiling like she was searching for divine inspiration. She didn't look like a school teacher as she was pretty, and she allowed her long blonde hair to fall over her shoulders. She wore tight jeans and boots, and the only school teachery thing about her was her dark glasses. They sat on her nose intrusively, making her look so much older than she actually was. Most of the boys held her in great regard, though, but sometimes when she was writing on the blackboard Collie and Danny O' Brien made rude gestures with their fingers. Collie said that he didn't fancy her much because she was flat chested, but I thought she was nice. I liked the way she spoke, and she was fierce intelligent.
'Well, Mr Collins, we are waiting,' she said.
'1951,' Collie said to general laughter.
'1951? Have you done anything to help Billy yet?'
'I have. I am researching the railway maps, Miss.'
'The maps?'

'Yeah, and the timetables, like.'

'Alright, we will see on Friday, I suppose, but it isn't fair to leave Billy do everything. Right. Anyone?'

'March 1961!' Danny O' Brien shouted.

'Alright, and why did they shut it down?'

'Because it was losin' stacks of money, Miss!'

'Yes, very good, Danny. It was losing money and it honestly was never going to see profit, so they took the decision to close it down. They didn't have much of a choice, did they?'

I was taken aback with the surety of her statement so I said, 'My Grandad says they were wrong, Miss. He told me to tell you that it was a mistake and a shame.'

'A mistake, Billy? How can he say that?'

Miss Forde leaned over on her desk like she felt she needed its support, her glasses slipping down her nose.

'He says everything has a cost, and the people could take the cost because the railway brought so much business to West Cork. That was what made it work. He says when they closed it down it broke the area, and it was against the wishes of the people they did it. He says it had no real need to make a profit.'

'Ah, Billy, your Grandad is living in the past. How can the tax payer support a failing enterprise? They had pumped thousands of taxpayers' money into the railway. It was losing more and more each year. The people who didn't want it closed hardly used it. Remember, Billy, that with the advent of the motor car, passenger numbers were declining. Business must make a profit. The taxpayer can't be bailing out failed enterprises.'

'Yes, Miss, but my Grandad says that it hurt West Cork so much that loads of other businesses failed too, and he reckons the passengers would have come back to the railway. The profit, he says, was in the service.'

'I think your Grandad may struggle a little with economic reality, Billy. We can chat again on Friday.'

Miss Forde left the desk and went to the blackboard and the two boys immediately started on the rude gestures, but she almost caught them when turning around quickly. She said to me, 'The days are long gone since the tax payer supported loss-making business, Billy. You tell your Grandad I said that.'

And I did, and he laughed at first. Then he turned to me smartly.

'She hasn't a clue; she's from a generation of illiterates!'

'She is very intelligent, Grandad,' I said.

He bellowed back, 'Intelligence is only of value when used wisely!' And off he went, leaving Niamh and me at the kitchen table.

'He is full of it,' Niamh said.

'Yeah, he said I should go see the captain.'

'Sure. The captain is half daft. What would you want with him?'

'Grandad reckons he could put me straight on the railways.'

'Hah. Grandad just wants you to chat to his drinking buddy. I can't see how the captain knows anythin' about the railway. He worked the ships when he was young. You go see him, Billy, but I wouldn't be hangin' on everythin' he says.'

'Alright, Niamh,' I said, 'but we have to have the project in by Friday, so I best be gettin' on with it.'

'You do that, boy. What you up to later?'

'Nothin'. Why, are you going out?' I said, because anytime Niamh was going out she asked me the same question.

'I dunno. I might go to the talent down in Holland's. You won't believe me, but Marty Burke is singing and playing his guitar.'

'Jesus, isn't he very loud?'

21

'Nah, just the ordinary guitar. You know he is very good, don't yah?'

'I heard he is handy.'

'I might go down with Mary Maher. She loves the music.'

'Fire away. Isn't Grandad at the active retirement over in Castletown? Sure, he won't be back till all hours.'

'I forgot about that, Billy. I will make up some sandwiches, or he will be complainin'. Do you want one?' Niamh went to the fridge hurriedly but she was in good form, whistling and then humming to herself.

'I can do egg and tomato or plain cheese. Hold on, I can do a few ham and cheese.'

'Ham and cheese for me. It will be faster, and I am starving.'

'Hungry chap, and you only after biscuits and tea!'

'I am a growing lad, Niamh. Anyway, I am off, out to see the captain. God knows how long he will keep me.'

'You are right. Don't let Frankie Holland bully you either. Tell him that it is school business if he gets smart.'

'I will.'

Niamh made lovely sandwiches, and she made mine first. All the time she was humming to herself, and I could sense that she had something up her sleeve that was making her happy. She gave me two ham and cheese and then another half sandwich when she saw how ravenous I was.

'You had better eat your dinner later, Billy.'

'No worries on that one,' I said confidently.

'You needn't wait up later, Billy. I won't be late, but you get to the bed with school in the mornin'.'

'I will be gone when you get back with him,' I said without thinking.

'With who?'

'I was thinkin' you might bring Marty back for a coffee.'

'I am not going out with him.'

'I know, Niamh, but you might bring him back just like you did before.'

I was on my feet at the kitchen door. She was looking at me incredulously.

'I will be in the bed, so.'

'I will not be bringing him back here, and if I did it would just be for a chat. The poor man is eatin' his heart out, so it might be best for me to have a chat with him!' she shouted after me.

I grabbed my jacket from the stand.

'Chat away so!' I shouted back and slid down the iron railing to the street.

The captain wasn't there. 'He won't be long,' Frankie Holland said. He gave me a fright, as I didn't see him hiding out in the narrow hall. The first thing I saw was his bald head peeping through, and then he brought the rest of his body. Frankie had a habit of standing straight and sticking out his chest if he was in good humour, and he also liked to talk if the mood was good. If he was quiet you knew that he was chewing something over, so he was best left. But he stuck his chest out for me.

'I saw him go up to the shop, so he won't be too long. Here, I will stand you a mineral, Billy. What is it?'

'I will have a diluted orange, Frankie, with ice if you don't mind.'

'Not at all. Isn't it a pleasure to have old Tom's grandson visit. Here, there's a bar of chocolate to go with it, and we will say nothin'.'

'Thanks.'

'Go over by the fire. That is where he sits, and sure as the fella said he will find you.'

'Grand fire, Frankie.'

'You know, Billy, the way things have gone, I spend most of my day stoking the fires. We have three fires goin', and

23

if I am not tendin' to one I am tendin' to the other. I have created a new job for myself because the pub business is dead and gone.'

And true to his word he was over with the bucket, shovelling slack onto what I regarded as a perfectly good fire.

'Keeps it down,' he said. 'I want it to burn but not for the night, as we have the talent later. That should do it grand, and the captain will be warm and it will be dead by nine. Billy, life is all about having a plan. Many fellas have a plan, boy, but very few of 'em stick to it.'

Frankie was gone again, bringing his bucket into the back lounge to tend to that fire. I wondered why he bothered as there was nobody in there, but then I figured that he just wanted to keep the place warm for himself. The captain limped in with his newspaper rolled up under his armpit; he paid no attention to me. He just walked to the bar. Resting against a stool he leaned over the counter searching for Frankie, but Frankie saw him from the back and shouted, 'Captain, the usual?'

The captain didn't reply; he just waved his fist in the air and walked over to the fire. He leaned over and deposited his newspaper on the seat beside me. Then he turned his back to warm his behind.

'Grand day, boy. Not summer yet but grand with it, even if the 'ast wind is still troublesome.'

I was about to say something but he intervened.

'Is old Tom away yet?'

'Ah, no, it is too early. They are goin' to Castletown for seven.'

'Seven,' the captain said, turning sideways. I could see his rough face clearly now, and the stubble of his black beard. He still had a full head of hair under his cap, and when he finally sat down I wanted to fold the collar of his jacket as he looked too warm so close to the heat.

24

'I am killed with the gout and my diabetes. It won't be the
heart that finishes me. It will be the diabetes, so the fuckin'
doctors say. But sure they could be makin' it up, hah?'
I noticed that his eyes were dark and still young looking
and it betrayed the rest of him, which looked lazy.
'Old Tom loves the active retirement, Billy. He keeps after
me to join, but, sure, there is nothin' active about me.'
I could smell something now. It wasn't off his skin,
because I could see that he was scrubbed. No, it was the
smell a fella gets when he hasn't changed his socks for an
age. It was strong one minute and weak the next, and
inexplicably my nose kept looking for it, for some reason it
was like I really wanted to smell it.
'Hot rum for the captain. Are you alright, boy, do you want
more chocolate?'
'Nah, I am grand out, Frankie, yah have me spoiled.'
'I hear you are the best of them, Billy,' he said walking
away.
'Old Tom has been singin' yer praises.'
'He has that,' the captain added.
'I try my best,' I said, laughing and thoroughly enjoying
myself. 'I wanted to ask you about the West Cork railway.
Yah see, we are doin' a project in school, and old Tom said
yah were the man to ask.'
The captain lowered his rum, and Frankie was busy filling
him a replacement. This time the captain didn't bother with
the hot water. He just took it neat. Frankie sauntered across,
and the captain grunted when he handed him the drink.
'I might go a pint of Murphy's too.'
Frankie went away to pull the pint.
'If that wind stays 'ast, we are in trouble!' the captain
shouted after him, and Frankie seemed to ignore him. But
then after a minute he looked up from behind the taps and
said loudly, 'It was east the other day, and I thought I was
going to die.' It was then I realised that these men had a

practised delay on their exchanges, and that one could
expect to have to wait for a reply to a comment. The
captain shifted uncomfortably in his chair, the fire
reddening the left side of his face. 'The railway was fucked
from the start, because it was the people that owneded it.'
I went to ask a question but the captain piped up with, 'My
father loaded the beet for many a year, and when the train
came the village went mad. It was a quare time, weren't it,
Frankie?'
''twas, even though I was only a child. God, the
excitement. It was the only way out of here, Billy.
People didn't have cars. No, there were no cars.'
'Jesus,' I said out of respect.
'Imagine, there were no cars!'
'Tell you, Billy, back then yah had to be somethin' to own
a car. I am not codding you.' Frankie said.
'His whole life was trains. He worked for the railway,
casual like, but he loaded the beet, and when he got paid he
came in here and got drunk, isn't that right, Frankie? He
would sit right where you are sittin', Billy. Spend half the
day here.'
'He would,' Frankie said, just in case I wasn't believing the
captain, 'ah, but it killed him, didn't it, when the railway
went. He never got any work after that. He never came in
then, Frankie. Used to sit in at home mopin' and cryin' to
himself. He was lost, boy,' the captain added ruefully.
'My father signed the petition to keep it open,' Frankie
said. 'Look at this photo, Billy.' On the wall by the door to
the back lounge was a large framed photograph. It was a
Sunday seaside excursion, and the crowds flocked from the
railway station. The street was full of eager day trippers,
people smiling and children running with excitement.
'I think the closing of the trains killed him, Sure, he never
worked another day in his life. It was all he knew, wasn't it.
He knew nothin' else, just trains and beet, and the loadin of

26

cattle, they even hauled seaweed boy. The odd time he helped unload the ships but that wasn't proper work, and they stopped that too.'

The captain paused, he had drunk most of his Murphy's. I was amazed. How could he lower a pint in three gulps? But he did, and Frankie had another one for him.

'Then there was the petition, and, God, the people had great hope. They all signed it, didn't they, Frankie?'

'They did. My own father signed it,' Frankie said, like we didn't hear him the first time.

'Remember how they used to bring us to the Regatta in Baltimore?' the captain asked finishing off his rum before starting on his pint.

'I do. I remember waiting for the train in Ballinascarty. Tell yah, Billy, thousands went. As a child I looked forward to it all the year, and my father, God bless him, never missed it.'

Frankie decided the fire needed a stoking again, and so he was on his hunkers doing the business. The captain watched him fascinated, and he waited till Frankie was finished before saying, 'on the last day, we expected a crowd. The crowd never came did it?'

'They did not. The people were pissed off, to tell you nothin' but the truth.' Frankie said.

The captain, looking me straight on, said, 'We took a ride on a railcar. We stayed on across the bridge in Timoleague, me and another few scuts. It was a pet day. We went on a few miles down the Argideen till the train stopped. The driver needed to piss and a few of the boys wanted to mess around in the river, so we hopped off the railcar and the Argideen cooled us down, the water was freezing boy, we all got wet.' The captain paused to reflect. 'I'll never forget us leavin' the pier for the last time. Movin' further away, till we finally lost sight of it. We thought we were great, but us poor divils had to walk all the way back soaking wet. Blisters on me feet. I was sore for weeks, boy.'

His eyes swelled with tears, and I saw his left hand tremble as he went to drink his pint. Frankie went back to the bar to pull him a fresh one whilst the captain steadied himself.

'I went to sea a few years later. I wasn't here when the old man died. It was a pity.'

'He got a great send-off, Captain, Sissy made sure of that. My father always said she gave him a great send off.'

'At least he got that,' the captain said.

*

Niamh was late in, and she was rushing around busy like a bluebottle. She made me an omelette, and she did chips in the chip pan the way I like them. But she didn't eat much herself; she said she had to go and get ready for the talent, and Mary Maher was a divil for bein' bang on time. I was tired and I was sore, 'cause she never asked me nought about the captain or how Frankie treated me. So I went off to the sitting room to watch the telly. I wanted to finish off the project, but to be honest I was sick of the trains and the sad stories about them. I still reckoned that despite all of the sentiment Miss Forde was probably right, and a business has to make money to survive no matter what. Mary Maher called bang on time, and she popped her head in to say hello. I was watching one of these "Cold Case" things, and it was just about to reveal the murderer when she came in.

'How's Billy, you are getting big!'

It wasn't like she always said that or anythin'. No, it was just the way she said it, like there was an undercurrent of *'Yer getting big, but to me you are still a kid'* about it.

'We are off to the talent.'

Mary was very plain whereas Niamh was really good looking. Collie always said that good-looking women had a habit of choosing plain-looking women for their friends, as it made them stand out and they were totally superior to

28

their pal. I don't know for sure if he is right but I did a sort of a survey for a week once, and, well, if he wasn't right then he wasn't far off it. Mary had a long nose and her face narrowed into it. She wore glasses, and she always had her hair tied back very severe like. She had a big tummy as well, but in fairness her worst attribute was that she was sour towards men, which didn't help.

'What time are you going to bed at?'

She was nosey too, which didn't go well with me.

'I dunno,' I said.

'Don't be late,' she said, like she was Niamh.

'I saw you comin' out of Holland's earlier. Did ya get a job?'

'I did not,' I said, turning up my "Cold Case."

She pretended to watch it for a second.

'No place for ya to be hangin' round so.'

'I wasn't hangin' round,' I said caustically.

'Oul lads in there. Nothin' for you, Billy. Only old men hangin' round doin' damn nothin'!'

'I told Niamh; I was goin' in about my project.' 'What project?' she quizzed.

Then Niamh arrived and gave me a sweet kiss on the forehead. Mary changed suddenly from being interrogator to misses nice.

'He is a sweetheart, Niamh,' she said.

'Don't be up late, Billy. I left you a dairy milk in the fridge.'

I loved the smell of Niamh when she was going out. It wasn't from the strong perfume she used, but she was scrubbed with some body wash and its residue stuck on the skin around her neck. She looked well in her new jeans and a real wool sweater.

'See you, Niamh!'

Mary glared at me so I said, 'Bye, Mam.'

'See you, Billy,' Mary said, and they were gone and I got bored with the television and I went to bed early, and I was thinking of trains and steam, and I imagined the train steaming through the valley by the Argideen, and I thought it was a wonderful sight. I must have slept for a while, but I did wake briefly to hear the sound of a man's voice in the kitchen, and I heard Niamh laughing and the man saying something, and her laughing again. It was too much for me to concentrate on and I still have no idea of the hour of the day, but it felt like it was late. I drifted off to a quiet sleep, but I have a distinct memory of a strong hand rubbing my head. I could tell it was a man's hand by the weight and the power of it, yet for all of its power it rubbed my head so gently.

The following morning Niamh was in great form over breakfast.

'Half day today. You know, I might go into Bandon and get myself a new outfit for Bridie's seventieth.'

'Is Bridie seventy?'

'She is.'

'So what would Nan have been?'

'Seventy. Wait, seventy-three. No, I am wrong, child. Seventy-four, poor creatur.'

'Seventy-four isn't old, is it? Grandad is older than that. Yah know, that's the advantage of being young, isn't it, Niamh? Like, barrin' an accident or somethin' dreadful, yah have all the years left to live. Very comfortin', isn't it? How did the talent go then?'

I was busy getting my lunch from the fridge and I put my schoolbag on the table to check on my books, and then I put the lunch in the side pocket.

'Marty Burke won it handy, like. He was brilliant. He sang his own song. There was no one to touch him. He was askin' after you. I said you were doin' grand, happy out with a long life ahead of you.'

'Thanks, Niamh. It is not that I want to live to be old, yah know. Only if I have all of my senses maybe. I would prefer to die young than be old and sick. I don't think the younger people wanna mind the old if they're sick, like.'

'What on earth makes ya say that?' Niamh said, getting up from the table to go to the sink where she went through the motions rattling mugs and plates.

'I dunno, I just thought it. Is Grandad havin' a lie in?'

'He is. The bus was very late. It was the early hours when they got back.'

'He will be jaded so.'

'I hope they had a good time,' Niamh said.

'Yah. The active retirement is great for him. It gets him out.'

'It does,' Niamh agreed.

'See you later,' I said.

'Take care!' Niamh shouted after me as I was halfway down the hall.

*

Collie hadn't added anything to the project, so I had tidied up the notes and went over them three times to check the spellings. I changed a few things. The last train from Courtmacsherry was the 31st of March 1961, but it wasn't a steam train. By then it was diesel, and I had better note that. We had one more day before presentation, and I dearly wanted to win first prize. Collie said that he wished the first prize was a date with Miss Forde, but it wasn't much. Just a voucher for Xtravision and your names on the school noticeboard. Still I wanted to win; it was no harm to have a competitive streak. Then I thought of Marty Burke winning the talent, and I wondered what it was like to win something like that. I had never won anything big as of yet.

Maybe I would never win anything. But then again maybe I would. Miss Forde interrupted my musings.

'So you have your project completed, Billy?'

'Yes, Miss.'

'Oh, good, anyone who has completed their project can hand it in today. It will give me more time to go through them, and we might even get to announce the winner tomorrow afternoon. Don't panic now, you still have 'til tomorrow morning, all you slackers!'

The class gave her a generous laugh. I looked at Collie who looked back at me blankly. So when Miss Forde appeared in front of our desk, I handed her the completed project. She took a minute to look over it and even turned to page two and then pages three and four. Danny O' Brien was the only other boy to hand his and Michael Donovan's in. Michael Donovan kept his head down like he was afraid that Miss Forde might ask him something, but she didn't.

'Well, Mr Collins, I expect you can stand up before the class and tell us all about the West Cork Railway.'

Collie smiled and threw his eyes to heaven.

'Thought not,' Miss Forde said.

'Billy will no doubt run us through it.'

The boys all laughed nervously, and Miss Forde returned to her desk satisfied.

*

Niamh gave me the wink. She always did when Grandad was out of sorts. He sat at the kitchen table nursing a mug of tea. It was my mug, but I didn't mind. He looked tired and worried. Niamh had returned from Bandon without her outfit. She hadn't found whatever it was that she wanted.

'Did you enjoy it anyhow?' she said to him.

'It was good, but they're a funny lot out there on the Beara. Clannish, ya know.'

'I would say so,' Niamh said.

'Billy, do you want tea?'

'I won't, I have a Coke in the fridge.' I went to get it.

'It was a long journey home. We couldn't get half of them out of the pub, but, sure, what of it? I was only moanin' 'cause I was sober. Someone had to be.'

Grandad sounded genuinely regretful about it all, and then he went quiet again.

'Have you homework, Billy?' Niamh said accusingly.

'I don't, because I handed in my project but most of the others aren't finished, so they got tonight to finish it.'

'Ya finished it?' Grandad asked.

'I did, and I saw the captain. Thanks, Grandad.'

'Ah, the captain. He has his troubles!'

'He does, alright,' Niamh said unnecessarily. 'Like, there are worse cases.'

'I have been thinkin',' Grandad said ignoring her.

'I was thinkin' I might move on. Like, it is lovely here, Niamh, and all, but Bridie's cottage is empty again, and it is a grand location, and in fairness to her, as you know she is hardly a favourite of mine, but she says I can have it for a song. I think I will accept her offer.'

Niamh looked at him, stunned.

'Yah mean move out, Father?'

'It will be for the best, Niamh. Let you and Billy have the place to yourselves.'

'I dunno,' Niamh said, sitting down.

'We will still see yah every day, like,' I said, trying to be positive.

'Ya will.'

'I dunno,' Niamh said again.

'It will ease yer workload, love,' Grandad said, and it was the first and only time I ever heard him refer to Niamh as "love," and I could sense that he was choking back the tears and he tried to hide his face by taking a sup of his cold tea.

'I will drop by to see you every day,' I said cheerfully. Now it was Niamh's turn, and she made no effort to be brave as the tears came a flowing.

*

I didn't think about it much that day because Collie called by with his football, and we went across the road to play three and in before it got dark. But the next day in class whilst Miss Forde was picking the project winner, I had a right rant about it in my head. Was old Tom moving out because he couldn't stand it anymore, like Niamh and me? Or was it all gone too tight, like the cottage wasn't big enough for the three of us? I couldn't figure it out, why he wanted to live on his own in the house where his dead wife was born and bred, like it was grand now and it was very central, like. Maybe it was the shorter walk to Holland's bar. Then I started thinking that all of the stuff that he said about the railway was right. Grandad knew his history, and what he had said not only made sense but it was the right thing for the people, and at the end of the day it was the people that mattered. I doubted that Grandad wanted to be nearer Holland's bar, mind you, but suddenly a worrying situation sprang to mind. What if Marty Burke wanted to move in with Niamh now? What would that mean? Would I have to play second fiddle to that fella, big and bold as he was? He might drive me mad with all of that song writing and singing, and because I looked like him everyone would think that I was his son. Now that could be an unmitigated disaster. Miss Forde broke my concentration. 'I think I have decided on the top two, so quiet now, boys. Danny and Michael, and Billy and Collie—or should I say Danny and Billy. But I won't go there, will I, class?' There was a general guffaw.

'Now Danny has gone to loads of trouble.' She held his presentation open. 'You see, he has pasted in loads of photos of the locomotives, and indeed some nice passenger photos. Danny—sorry, they have also put in some lovely maps of the railway line, and I like this, Danny's granny's personal account of a journey from Cork to Dunmanway. Very nice. But what I really like about this one is the comparison they make between the West Cork Railway and modern times. Making the point of how wasteful much of our public services are. Very true.'

Miss Forde looked over the class expecting a reaction, but when there was none she said, 'Nine out of ten! Well done, Danny and Michael!' She continued. 'Billy and Collie, again, very good detail on the line with maps and even a timetable. I like that, Collie.' Again the boys all laughed. 'Lovely photos and an interesting take on economics from Billy's Grandad.' The boys laughed loudly. But I was having none of it, putting up my hand. 'The closure of the West Cork Railway did untold economic damage to this region, Miss. No matter what anyone says, it did terrible damage to communities. Not everythin' makes sense all the time, like.' There was general quiet. Miss Forde smiled down at me.

'Seven out of ten,' she said.

On the way home I got to thinking about life, and, sure, it was no wonder that people are daft, including me. If Marty Burke moves in on top of me and poor Niamh, all the village tongues will be wagging. Sure, they will think we threw poor old Tom out so that Niamh can have her lover man with her all of the time. Another thing that was becoming abundantly clear was that I had an urgent need to smarten up. In the new world that Miss Forde lived in, there was no room for creative thinkers like me. No, it was dog eat dog, and everything was based on the notion of profit, even if it didn't make any long-term sense.

I could see the long road into my future. Maybe I would live in Cork or Dublin or even London. I will be a high flyer, because now I understand the rules even though I don't agree with them or even think they might really work. Nah, I was sure of it. I would beat them all and be the worst of them if it needs be.

THEY ALL RAN AFTER THE FARMERS WIFE

'You look shocked.'

'It's been a long time, Marianne,' Lillian said.

'Five years is a long time.'

'Six years. It's six years now.'

'Wow. How time moves on, eh?'

Marianne tried hard to smile.

'You haven't changed, Lillian, not a bit of you. So what do you think?'

'What do I think?

'Yes, it is a legitimate question. What you do think, Lillian?'

'I see. What do I think? I think you look crap, and I am shocked to be honest. At first I hardly recognised you. It's been too long.'

'It has,' Marianne said, turning her wheelchair towards the window. Lillian followed her. The view was over playing fields that were waterlogged with random pools and single gulls dancing. Beyond a minor road that was tree lined, cars passed with their sidelights on.

'Six months. Maybe not even that,' Marianne said quietly.

'My God, are they sure?'

'I don't think they would make a mistake, do you?'

Marianne leaned over like a child seeking affection and Lillian, placing her hand on her head, patted her softly.

'My uncle was given a week to live, but he lived three months.'

'Lillian, when you have what I have you don't want to live. It gets progressively worse. I am having a good day today; normally the pain is terrible and I can't function. To be honest, if you really hate someone then wish multiple sclerosis on them. A greater curse you couldn't ask for.'

'Six months,' Lillian said.

'We haven't seen each other for six years, and you will be dead in six months. My God.'

'I have been dead for a good time now, Lillian. The last two years have been the worst. I don't know how I'd've managed without Sheila. She comes to see me every day.'

'Sheila. She was always so kind. Like underneath all that feminist ranting and the rage, there really was a person.'

'I won't hear a bad word about Sheila. And by the way there was nothing between us, before you start asking. We just became good friends, that's all. Do you know, she has a man in her life now. Not a bad catch either. Some fella she met through work. I think he works for the Times, but I might be wrong. It could be one of those English rags.'

Lillian went to sit on the sill where she could see Marianne face on. The disease had ravaged her, removing all the fat from her cheeks. Her eyes had caved in so much they were no longer worthy of the name. These were tiny lights lost in deep flawed sockets.

Even her voice had changed. Marianne always had a gay lilt, but now her voice was deep and singular like a man.

*

Six years earlier

It was Marianne who knew Diane Ashley. Marianne had rented a cottage on the edge of the estate. It wasn't much; just two rooms up and two down with a kitchenette. She loved it, as she could paint and rest and then paint again. She never tired of the view over Coolmain and the sandy beach at Harbour View. Diane Ashley had allowed her to have the place for a nominal rent as Marianne was good with horses, and she helped out around the stables in the mornings. Sometimes she rode out with her landlord. They would cross the estate and on through the woods before bringing the horses down to Coolmain and along the sands at low tide. After some time Diane Ashley took to calling for coffee, and then this elevated into a regular lunch and eventually copious glasses of wine.

Marianne had always fancied that she would get married someday, yet the pleasures of men had sort of passed her by as she spent many years nursing elderly parents. But she knew that she was good looking, mind, as her mother had gone to great trouble to tell her so, and then she placed Marianne's photographs all over the family home so many that she even grew to admire herself after time. Diane Ashley was a beautiful woman, but like many women who live around horses she sort of became horsey, like. To be fair, if she were a horse she'd have been a handsome one with a long mane. For a woman of forty-two she kept herself well. She wore expensive sports gear when riding, but when she was socialising she was radiant with an array of dresses and frocks that were visually stunning. Yet if she dressed down and wore jeans with boots she looked just as elegant. When she came in for lunch, Marianne would marvel at the way she brushed her auburn hair back from her shoulders and how it managed to stay there.

'I really must ask Joseph to fix the fence out by the road. We will lose cattle or, worse still, someone will lose their life. We have so many workmen and yet something like that can go weeks without attention, beggar's belief.'

'What hole? Diane, is there a hole?'

'Yes, over by the road at the corner. Didn't you see it?'

'No, I didn't.'

'We rode right by it this morning. Marianne, you need to get your eyes checked. Ah, maybe it's just me. I am always on the lookout for these things. I must drive Joseph mad. But believe me he deserves it, he is so lax. It comes from being hardly ever here. He has the manager do everything, and between you and me I don't think that fellow is worth a damn. He is too surly as well. You ask him to do something

and he just sort of looks at you, you know? Like he is
thinking.'
"Who the hell is she to ask me, Mr Farm manager, to do
anything." Honestly!'
'Is that coffee too strong?' Marianne asked.
'No, it is fine. I do hope this weather keeps up for a few
days. The horses love bein' out, makes such a difference.
The bloody rain has me worn out.'
'I got these rolls in Timoleague in the supermarket. They
look delicious, don't they? And I bought the ham in Clon.
Help yourself to everything, Diane, don't be shy.'
'Really, you are too good, spoiling me like this.'
'Spoiling you? Diane, how many lunches have you given
me? I can't count.'
'That's Mrs Ball. You know she has a fit if I go into the
kitchen. It's a bit rich, seeing that it's my kitchen, but she is
so good. Obtuse but good. Joseph can't stand her. He says
she is a vampire. He refuses to go anywhere near her, but as
you know she is a genius so I keep her. Cheers!' Diane
raised her coffee cup and then drank a little but she only
picked at her roll, which irked Marianne as she had gone to
great trouble buying it all. She had made sure the rolls were
super fresh and the ham was the finest. She had made the
coleslaw herself, but then Diane said, 'I wonder, is the lad
back with the horses? You know, he is a strange fellow too.
I think that he is good with them overall, but he can't ride
for nuts. But there you have it.'
She took a bite of her roll and drank more coffee, much to
Marianne's relief. When the meal was over Marianne took
a bottle of Chardonnay from the fridge.
'Oh, lovely,' Diane said, looking closely at the label.
Marianne spun the bottle towards herself, opening it
quickly and pouring. She almost filled the tumbler.
'Enough,' Diane pleaded, but Marianne continued filling it
to the brim. Diane took a sip to steady the glass.

'Delightful, my dear. By the way, have I told you about my new friend, Sheila?'

'No,' said Marianne, filling her own glass.

'Sheila Walsh. She writes for the Times and the Independent and loads of other magazines. I met her at a function over in Inchadoney. I have to admit, I couldn't stand her at first. You know, she is one of these short-haired man types. No makeup. Not a brush. She dresses like a man too. But she made a speech—I can't remember what it was for—oh, yes, sorry, it was for the SVP. And she gave this speech about the poor and the new homeless, but my God she let the men have it, Marianne. She used the word fuck about four times. I thought they were going to shut off the mike!'

'Lovely hotel, Inchadoney,' Marianne said. Diane looked at her for a moment before saying,

'Then she was going on, like this was afterwards, about sex, and how women were slaves to men, and women should seek out other women for sex and empower themselves and not be serving men. I thought she was mad, to be honest.'

'Sounds funny,' Marianne said.

'How did she go down?'

'I dunno. One or two people were laughing, but she got a great clap and there were crowds around her afterwards like everyone wanted to talk to her. I suppose she is a minor celebrity. She is always on the television and on the radio. She is very well known.'

'Her father was a lecturer in Trinity when I was there, but he drank.'

'I didn't know you were in Trinity.'

'I did my masters on the history of art,' Marianne said proudly.

'Did you now?' Diane made her voice even more posh as she rubbed Marianne's left arm.

'Well, now, I would want to mind myself I didn't realise that I was in the company of an intellectual.' Marianne went puce.

'I went back as a mature student. The kids were all looking at me, an oul wan in her thirties, but I did it, and I did well, I hope.' Marianne drank more wine to settle herself.

'What do you think of all of this woman-with-women stuff? Is there anything in it? You know, we never had kids. Joseph couldn't after his cancer you know, but I wonder what it's like. Do you?'

'No,' blurted Marianne.

'I know I sound awful, dear, but this woman, Sheila Walsh, she has me thinking. Anyhow I invited her over for lunch on Saturday, and it's great because Joseph is in Dublin at the rugby. So we will have the house all to ourselves. Promise you will come, Marianne. I am afraid she might proposition me if I entertain her alone.'

After they drank all of the wine Diane offered to help with the dishes, but Marianne insisted that there was no need. Anyhow Diane was a little tipsy and she even suggested ringing the lad and have him fetch more wine from her cellar, but Marianne managed to persuade her that it was too early as she wanted to paint, especially on such a bright afternoon. Marianne watched Diane walk the grassy lane. She turned back twice to wave needlessly before disappearing down the pathway through the wood.

*

'You realise that men dominate politics, and if we replaced all of those old party hacks with women
we might get things done. It isn't that men are illogical, Diane, it's more that women are not as corruptible. We don't have this culture, you know. Back slapping, big fucking car, a round of golf, a few whiskies and how's your father. They keep feeding us lies like "The older men get,

43

the wiser they become." I think that is fucking nonsense. They just became comfortable within the corrupt world they have created.

'I see Marianne looking at me. I don't hate men, my darling. I just hate what they do to us. They disempower us at every turn in politics and at home. In the workplace, in every aspect of our existence, surely it's time for women to get up off of their arses and tell them to fuck off.'

Diane looked at Marianne who tried to distract herself by reaching for her wine glass. Sheila meanwhile lowered hers, not bothering to leave a respectable drain at the bottom.

'Welcome to women's liberation. Burn the bra, girls. Time to put up or shut up. No more nonsense; the revolution has started. Instead of a man's world, it is a woman's world!'

It was the first time that Marianne saw Diane's look; she gazed at Sheila as she ranted in full flight. Diane couldn't keep her eyes off of her. Marianne felt that she was counting the words as they left Sheila's mouth.

After lunch Diane brought them for a short stroll in the garden, and though it was February the evenings had taken an hour of a stretch and the plants and flowers were discussing the forthcoming spring.

'Outside of procreation why do we need men?' Diane said suddenly.

'Men are physically stronger, Diane. We can't argue with that, can we?' Marianne commented.

'Come now, girls, I am not competing with men. To tell you the truth I quite like men, they can be kind of straight up you know, whilst we girls are kind of enigmatic and we are terrible bitches. I will never compete with men on their patch, my love. No, my quarrel with them is an intellectual one. I am not inferior, get me?'

'Yes, Sheila, but I was thinking more of the body than the mind,' Diane said. She brought them down a grass bank and onto the path that led to the stables.

'It is the eternal conundrum, isn't it? Wait till you see, Diane. I will start painting nude women next, and I will subliminally study the repressed sexual emotions of women.'

'I will model for you, Marianne,' Diane said loudly, and Sheila dropped a pace falling behind. When they reached the stable yard she wandered to the stable doors to pet the curious horses that inspected the afternoon. They sneezed and made shrill noises throwing their heads about.

'Are you serious, Diane? Would you like to pose for me?'

'I will, Marianne. Nothing I would like better.'

And so it began. Diane called every Tuesday, and after lunch and a few glasses of wine they went upstairs to the makeshift studio overlooking the beach at Coolmain. Marianne was never happy with the paintings that she did for Diane, and it wasn't so much that she was disappointed with her own efforts. It was more that Diane ruined them by trying to look sultry and flashing her breasts. What bothered her most was that Diane was actually wonderful in reality, but it was impossible to capture that in her paintings. She always felt that she had failed spectacularly in her quest to represent the living reality that was the beautiful Diane, and Diane knew it. Whilst she would openly praise the work, Marianne always felt a certain reticence from her and she never offered to buy any of the paintings either. There was one that stood out, and that was one of Diane lying naked on the sofa draped with a white sheet from her left shoulder over her breast and all the way down to her toes. Diane lay on her right side with her head away. It was sturdy, and her bottom protruded to give the work a robust feel. It was Diane who had made the first move, and Marianne laboured over it for days. Diane wasn't too forward, just a gentle kiss. Then she started to call more regularly and invite Marianne to go places with her, places she used to go to before but always alone, like art events in Clon where the American artist, Maggie Ryan, gave lectures on art and animation. Marianne was at once flattered and also terrified by Diane's attentions, whilst she was happy to get more intimate and altogether closer, she was unsure of any physical attraction that may lead to a sexual encounter. She hadn't felt any strong sexual desire as of yet, and when Diane had kissed her it was rather platonic. One afternoon after they had visited Maggie Ryan's gallery and listened to her monotonous American drawl, they arrived back at the cottage for wine as Marianne was too tired to work.

'I think that girl is a little mad,' Diane announced.

'What makes you say that?' Marianne was opening the wine bottle.

'Here I am, patron of the arts, known far and wide as the queen of Kilbrittain, and she spends all of her time talking to you and deliberately ignoring me, and anything that I had to say to the point of being rude. I mean, I know you are both artists, but artists need people like me, or they won't eat. By the way, I thought some of her work was hideous and out of kilter.'

'Ah, that's just her animation, Diane. She distorts things on purpose, you know. I see what you mean about her. She can be a little rude and intense, but she is very talented all the same.'

'I dunno. She will starve if she needs my money.'

Marianne poured the wine and Diane drank a mouthful, looking at her intently.

'Nowhere near as good as your work, my dear. I can't say that I take to this animation. Isn't life distorted enough without artists making it worse?'

'Maybe.' Marianne laughed. Diane leaned over and kissed her full on the lips.

'You are, my darling Marianne.' Marianne felt Diane's hands clasp the back of her neck and then draw her in. She tasted the wine from her soft wet lips, and she pushed her lower body into hers. Suddenly Marianne felt a rush of excitement, but she whispered,

'I dunno about this, Diane.'

'It's ok, my dear, it is what I want. It is what I have longed for.'

Following Diane's kiss many afternoons were spent in Marianne's bed. Diane loved to bring a chilled bottle of white wine upstairs with them with a wine glass placed carefully on each locker, and after love making she would sit up propped by a pillow and chat incessantly. After time Marianne got used to the ritual and the pleasure that came with it. She read books on the subject and soon realised that it wasn't anything to do with her sexual identity but rather much more about sexuality itself, as she didn't in reality have any previous sexual experience. So she grew to love it and then she longed for it, and when Diane couldn't come over she mourned for her and missed her to the point of distraction. Sometimes she could lose herself in her work, but other times she just sat drinking wine and crying. And after three months had passed and all the barriers had been broken, she started to obsess over her new love. If Diane failed to come over, Marianne would call her on her mobile and get mad.

'But you said that last time, Diane. You can't keep making excuses.'

Diane would mutter something, keeping her hand over the receiver and then say gently,

'Hey, honey, you know I am busy. I told you this week was manic. Joseph is in London, and I have the show jumping and I have to go to the women's conference for Sheila. She needs me to go.'

'Why not bring me?' Marianne said.

'Because you don't like Sheila. You find her loud and rude, remember? Look, honey, I will call by the weekend. I have to go.' She was gone and Marianne cried bitterly, spending the afternoon alone. It was so unfair, now that summer was in full flight, to be left alone whilst the love of her life fraternised with what was after all half a man.

On these lonely days she took to walking Coolmain alone in the evenings. The beach was usually pretty empty but there were always a few stragglers here and there. The usual dog walkers or mothers with kids, but she was glad of the walk as it gave her space to think, and in the distance she could see people walk the beach at Harbour View. It was much busier, and the channel flowing into Kilbrittain Creek was clear and the fast rush of the water cheered her. Often she would look out over the ocean and admire the lines of trees that covered Wood Point. It was on one of these walks that she decided to confront Diane about their relationship, like what was it that she wanted? Was it just a sexual affair, or did she truly love her and was there a hope that despite Joseph that they could share a life together? Then Marianne chided herself for being so foolish. Who was she fooling? Diane Ashley was married and her husband was one of the biggest farmers in the district. How would she give all that up? For what? For a foolish struggling artist who lived on the breadline? Hardly now, she concluded, but still she needed to thrash it out, and she convinced herself that she would very soon.

But the next time Diane called all of her urgency dissipated as Diane was full of chat over lunch, talking incessantly about her new horses and urging Marianne to join her for an early morning gallop over the sands. When they drank their wine Diane got a little mellow.

'I was wondering if you could have a look at Joseph's laptop. We have left it into that fellow over in Timoleague twice, but the bloody thing is still acting up.'

'What's the matter with it?'

'Dunno really. Something to do with going on and offline without warning, you know. It's vital for him, you know, when he is checking out bloodstock. Do you know, we have one hundred cows as of today? One hundred, Marianne, and we started out with fifty.'

'Wow!'

'Not bad, and they say we're in recession. You see the coping classes keep the chin up!'

Diane laughed, but Marianne didn't quite get the joke. She wanted to say, that's all well and good when you inherit a hundred-acre estate, but she didn't as Diane was in a good mood and somehow it lifted her own spirits.

'Bring it over; I will have a look at it. My broadband isn't great, but I am handy with the old laptops.'

'Do your best. I am sure we can afford a new one, but why waste? I will send the lad over with it later. God, I am tired today. It's all the early mornings; bloody horses never lie in!'

Afterwards they made tender love, and Marianne felt that Diane was particularly passionate. When she did her usual propping-up-her-pillow-and-chatting Marianne stayed flat, her head barely visible above the sheets and the duvet. She lay on her side looking up at Diane who sat unashamed exposing her breasts.

'I was thinking I might commission you to paint Sheila.
Oh, I don't mean in the nude. Hah, no, that wouldn't do
now. No, I want you to paint her like serious, with a serious
expression on her face, like you just caught her whilst she
was pontificating on one of those TV political shows.
Could you do that?'

'I dunno. I have never done anything like that, Diane.'

'I want to auction it for the Lions Club you know. I bet if I
gave you a few thousand I would get five grand for it at
auction, which is net three for the charity. Am I mad?'

'Probably,' Marianne said lazily.

'How do I catch her, like, in the middle of a rant? I
presume you want me to work off of film or stills. She is
hardly likely to model for me in ranting mode, is she?'
Marianne laughed heartily. Diane, looking hurt, said,

'I thought it was a win-win. You know, you getting work,
Sheila getting publicity, and the Lions Club making money.
But if you are not interested...' Diane faked annoyance.
She pulled up the duvet to cover her breasts, as it was chilly
with the window open.

'You see a lot of her, Diane.'

'And?'

'And I am jealous.'

'Don't be.'

'Easy for you to say, Diane. It is little me left here pining
for you.'

'Well, little you needs to get a life. I like bein' around
Sheila. She is interesting and radical and very alive. She
gives me lots of ideas and food for thought. So what's
wrong with that, dear? Am I not allowed friends? This is
worse than a jealous husband.'

'I didn't mean it like that!'

'How did you mean it?'

'Not like that.'

'That's the way you come across, Marianne, jealous.'

'I can't help loving you.' Marianne placed her hand on Diane's right breast.

'I can't change how I feel.' Diane removed her hand forcefully and turned to face the window.

'I am free now. For the first time in my adult life, I feel free to make whatever choices I like. I love you too, Marianne, but don't pressure me to be a certain way. I am who I am, alright? I can't be who you want, not all of the time. Give me space, please, do.' Marianne sat up in the bed, worried that she had gone too far. She straightened the pillow behind her head and sighed.

'I will paint her if that's what you want.'

'That's what I want,' Diane said.

The lad dropped the laptop over but not till the following morning, and Sheila rang to say that she would drop by with DVD'S of some television shows for Marianne to study. Diane didn't call for lunch that day as promised, and the food Marianne had bought went to waste. It was a dull wet summer's day, and Marianne watched as a young mother battled the wind and the rain to get her two children onto the beach with their raincoats and wellies. Yet somehow the kids seemed to love it.

*

It wasn't a good summer. It rained most of the time, and when it didn't rain it was dull. The sky was grey, and only occasionally the wind blew and at least allowed some respite. On this day Marianne studied the clouds and over the ocean they were like giant Arctic peaks, snow-covered mountains sweeping across the sky. Then Diane called unexpectedly, disturbing her concentration.

'I came to thank you for the laptop. Such a dear, and to think it was something that simple after all. I am useless with these things, but Joseph was really pleased.' Marianne said nothing, putting on the kettle and shifting the bread bin as it was too close to the lead.

'I can't stay, dear. I must dash, actually. Sheila is speaking in UCC, and I wouldn't miss it.'

'Is she?'

'She is debating rather, with that professor fellow. You know the one that says women should stay at home and mind their kids and keep house. He was on the radio the other day giving out about the SUVs and the school runs. The man is mad. He was on about crèches and playschools being a total disaster for women and children. Did you ever? I hope Sheila gives him a good bashing.'

'That's yer man James Doyle. He is a creep. If he had his way, Diane, we would all be destitute, living in trees, swinging from one to the other.'

Marianne didn't laugh, as it wasn't her intention to be funny. Diane just smiled at her and turned to go.

'Diane, wait a second.'

Diane turned back to her friend. She was still smiling, but it had started to wear off.

'I have something to tell you about the laptop.'

'Yeah?'

'He needs a new one. That one is on its last legs.'

'I will tell him, but he is as mean as dishwater and he tells me that he prefers the office computer anyway. See you!'

Diane was gone and Marianne made herself coffee. She sat at the kitchen table waiting for it to cool as it was too hot. Maybe she should have just come out and said it, but how do you tell someone like Diane that her husband has disturbing images on his laptop? She had found them quite by accident. She had gone into a folder that was clearly marked cattle. It was a fluke as she was just checking something, and she was in fact really bored, and she wondered what all the fuss was about cows, and perhaps she may learn something. There it was: hundreds of images. It was disgusting and vile, and how any man could contemplate viewing such stuff appalled and upset her. But she couldn't bring herself to tell Diane.

That afternoon she met Maggie Ryan for coffee in Clon. Maggie was late as usual. She walked into the coffee shop pulling her handbag up over her shoulder. She hit against two tables on her way as the passageway was too narrow, and she cursed as she brushed against a third before she got to sit.

'Goddamn place is like a cage. You think they might leave us some room. They want to fit as many people in as they can squeeze, but this fucking place is always empty. I can't get into it without nearly killing myself. Fuck sakes, is she here yet?'

'Who?'

'Lillian.'

'Who?'

'Lillian, the art student. I was telling you about her. She is very good, but her animation is shit. You might like her, Marianne, because she does good seascapes. Well, good for her, I mean. Fuck this.'

Maggie was on her feet, and she shuffled her way to the deli counter. She asked the young assistant for a coffee and a slice of chocolate cake, and then she turned to Marianne.

'Do you want more coffee? How about some cake?'

'I am ok,' Marianne said.

'Tell me you are watching your weight, and I will shoot you. You are hardly there. A slice of chocolate cake would be the makings of you.' Maggie walked back to the table lazily, still brushing off of tables and cursing under her breath.

'I am fucking sick of painting anyways. Chocolate cake is so much better, but this coffee is muck, shit like dishwater.'

'I forgot about Lillian. That's good that she's coming,'
Marianne said meekly,
'Yeah, well, she is totally gorgeous, but she is probably a
dyke, you know. I think she hit on me, but I always think
that. I always think men are hitting on me too.'
Maggie smiled and Marianne sensed that she was just
having fun with her such was the glint in her eye. She
watched as Maggie took a huge bite of her cake and
allowed the crumbs to fall randomly. Marianne looked
around her nervously whilst Maggie still held the half-eaten
slice of cake in her mouth.
'I was wondering if I should tell someone something about
someone else, you know?' Maggie looked at her without
expression.
'I mean someone who is close to someone that I care for
deeply.' Maggie put the remainder of her cake back on the
dish, and she stared at Marianne blankly.
'How fuckin' close is the person that's close?'
'Husband.' Marianne waited for a reaction but Maggie just
started to eat her cake once again, making more of a mess.
'Fucking coffee is piss. I am going to send it back. I tell
you, my darling, you don't ever tell a wife anything about
her husband. She will fucking kill you.'
She was up shuffling her way to the counter. Marianne
expected her to tear into the girl serving but she didn't. She
just said something, and the girl smiled and poured her
some fresh coffee. Then Lillian walked in, and Marianne
looked on speechless. She was in her late twenties, a
natural blonde. She was tall, and Marianne loved her
gabardine coat that was wet at the lapels. The rain shower
had passed over, and when she came over Marianne was
smitten by her deep blue eyes that stared intently from
beyond a button nose.
'Marianne!' Lillian said, patting Maggie on the shoulder.
'Cake! You are a rascal. What about the diet?'

54

'Fucking diet can wait. I am fucking starving. Anyways I love chocolate cake but the coffee is piss, I warn you.'

'Hello, Lillian,' Marianne said suddenly nervous.

'I can get you a coffee. I haven't got long, I have to be back by two, and I was twenty minutes in the bank. They don't mind keeping you waiting.' Lillian turned to go to the counter, but Marianne said, 'Did you bring me anything to have a look at?'

'No,' Lillian said, looking suspiciously at Maggie who was letting the last of the crumbs fall from her hand.

'I never told her you would bring anything. Anyways, aint we going to drive by to see her at the weekend? No big deal.' Maggie looked at Marianne, her chocolate cake consumed. She looked satisfied.

'Yeah, I am going to call by. Maybe Saturday?' Lillian said, still looking anxiously at the counter.

'Saturday is good,' Marianne said, 'in the afternoon.'

'Oh,' Lillian said, looking distressed.

'I work in the afternoons. Is morning no good at all?'

'Christ, you two are fucked up. Just say eleven-thirty, Marianne, and she will be there. I know, because I will drive her. The child can't drive yet.' Lillian stared at Marianne, awaiting her reaction.

'Eleven-thirty then.' Marianne smiled and watched as Lillian went to order her coffee, and she saw how elegantly she moved. She watched her chat with the friendly girl at the counter, ordering an open sandwich, and Marianne loved the way that she leaned over to inspect it as the girl put it on a plate and then gave her some paper napkins.

*

Diane had phoned to make her excuses, and when Marianne put the phone down she saw Maggie's car turn in from the road. She drove a beat-up Mazda that was dinged all over the bonnet. It chugged to a halt, and Marianne watched as Lillian got out first. Then Maggie clambered out the driver's side cursing under her breath and dropping her keys, and when she bent over to pick them up she just missed hitting her head off the swinging door by an inch. She didn't even notice; she just kept talking and then bending over again to get stuff from the back seat. Lillian noticed her at the window. At first she tried to evade her stare, but then she relaxed and looked on at Marianne steadily. It was Marianne who blushed and went to the front door where she just opened it and stood watching.

'I can't find that fucking book I promised you. You know, I swear I put it in with the other stuff, but Christ if it isn't there.'

'Maybe it fell under the seat,' Lillian said, throwing her eyes to heaven.

'I looked under the fucking seat,' Maggie said but decided to look once again.

'Don't worry about it.' Marianne smiled at Lillian, who showed her perfect teeth when she smiled back.

'I will get it from you some other time.

'The fuck if I didn't put it in here!'

Maggie was gone again, searching the rear of the car.

Lillian, sick of waiting, came to Marianne.

'I brought some stuff for you to look over.' Marianne took the rolls of canvas from her. She was tempted to look at them there and then, but she decided to wait.

'Coffee, guys, we can have elevenses at midday. How's about that?'

'Sounds good,' Lillian said, and then Maggie found the book.

'It was in the fucking glove compartment. Would you fuckin' credit that? I must have shoved it in there because I knew I put it on the damn seat, but when I collected this one I must have shoved it in.'

'Have a coffee,' Marianne said.

56

'I got some teacakes over in Barryroe yesterday. Come on, you two, settle in. Just move those magazines.' Lillian moved the magazines from the kitchen chair as Marianne instructed.

'Now we can relax, and then I will have a look at your work.' Lillian smiled, once again showing her perfect teeth. 'This is a lovely cottage!'

Marianne, handing her a coffee, said, 'It's fine for me. Not too big to clean, and yet big enough to lose myself in.'

'She gets it for nothing. Marianne is good at getting stuff for nothing.' Maggie grabbed a teacake. She removed the paper casing quickly before taking an enormous bite, and then speaking with her mouth full, she spat, 'She is well in with the owner, gets to ride out horses, all posh like. Not like fuckin' me, poor as fuck. I don't get benefactors.'

'If I only had your talent,' Marianne said seriously.

'Talent has fuck all to do with it,' Maggie said, stuffing the rest of her teacake in her mouth and swallowing half of her coffee to wash it down.

'I can have all of the fucking talent in the world, but if I aint got money I am screwed. So you are best off with your benefactor, even if she is a stuck-up bitch.'

Lillian got up and walked across the room to the bay window. She was quiet for a second. Marianne watched her as she surveyed the scene over Coolmain.

'She has a millionaire's view as well, the lucky bitch.' Maggie looked at Marianne mischievously.

'Wonder what she has to fuckin' do just to hold on to this place. It is a chore, I bet.'

Maggie pushed the table away from her chair as an indicator that she was finished. Lillian turned round suddenly.

'I have painted it already. It is very beautiful, Marianne. Like, it is not that it's wild at all, but it is more that it is calm and on the surface it isn't dramatic, but that is a

57

mistake, isn't it, as in essence it couldn't be any more dramatic, could it?'

Marianne stared across the room paralysed. It wasn't the eloquence or the soft lilt of her voice. It wasn't even the blonde coldness of her, but it was the passion she espoused. It came from somewhere deep within her soul.

After time Marianne realised that Lillian wasn't much of an artist. It was a fact that her seascapes were good, but she was in all truth only average. She did good clouds and waves, but her work lacked depth and she was lazy. Often her canvas was unfinished as she hurried her work, so anxious was she to present it. Marianne never told her the truth, and she collected Lillian twice a week so as she could tutor her. For a time she was a good attentive pupil, returning each week with an improved canvas, and she lapped up any praise that Marianne bestowed on her. After countless sessions Marianne all but lost interest in her as a prodigy as she had in fact fallen for her hook, line, and sinker, so much so that art had just become an excuse to see her. Soon she found herself planning trips to exhibitions all over the county accompanied by Lillian, she just loved being close to her, and this also gave her an opportunity to gauge Diane's mood to see if she was in anyway jealous. But she seemed happy with her partner's newfound freedom, and she always arranged to go see or entertain Sheila Walsh when Marianne was busy. The main problem for Marianne was that Lillian had no earthly idea as to her feelings for her, and although Marianne suspected that Maggie had divulged all about her private life she couldn't be sure. The question was how she could open up to Lillian about her true feelings for her. Many a morning lying in her bed she thought of how shocked Diane would be to learn that she had acquired a new and beautiful lover. How jealous and tormented she would be. But in truth whilst she sorely wished for it, she hadn't quite got through to Lillian. Action was needed if she wasn't to allow it all slip through her fingers. Thus she gave herself an ultimatum: the weekend of the Courtmacsherry festival. This was it. She had to tell Lillian how she felt about her and accept the consequences. She also had to accept that Diane was over; she hadn't called by for weeks, and she spent all of her free time with Sheila now.

Marianne set off to meet with Lillian, full of trepidation, driving up the hill and passing the Pink Elephant restaurant. She would have loved to stop for a drink but there was no time, taking the tight turns, and then on to the coast road with a view of Courtmacsherry village on the far side of the estuary. The trees on Wood Point fluttered in the wind, and rain clouds followed coming from the Atlantic. The road was quiet and suddenly she started to worry as to what she should do about Joseph, if anything at all. Was it all not a little irrelevant now that Diane was fading from her life? As she passed through Timoleague the seawater swished against the wall beneath the abbey, and the view down the estuary relaxed her. There was no need to do anything about Joseph now; that dream was dead. It was time to move on to more exciting things. Lillian was waiting for her in the Golden Pheasant coffee house, and she ordered two coffees as Marianne took a chair.
'Where are they putting you?'
'Upstairs. Marianne, I thought you fixed that for me.'
'Upstairs here is good but they are using the Lifeboat station, so that might be better. I dunno, mine are in the Pier House but I do that every year.'
Marianne stopped as she didn't want to give any impression of superiority.
'I will swap with you, Lil. It will give you a boost. To be honest they might get lost here. I dunno.'

'Whatever you think,' Lillian said.

'Would you like a scone? They look nice.' Marianne shook her head.

'I won't, I had a good breakfast.'

Lillian, looking at her knowingly, said, 'I think I might have room for one. I just had a cup of tea and a slice of stale toast, so I will.'

'Go ahead. I will go up to the Pier House in a minute and get them to change mine with yours.'

'Ah, Marianne, there is no need.'

'Every need, my dear. We must help our younger artists.'

'I wish.'

'Well, you are young,' Marianne said.

'A few years on you, but sure what does age matter? Do you think I might sell something? I could do with the money. The job is drying up at the end of the month.'

'I hope so, but don't worry, I will look after you.' Marianne wasn't sorry that she said it but she was a little worried, as she didn't want to let the cat out of the bag too soon. Lillian looked at her quizzically.

'It would make my life to sell something, Marianne, it really would.'

'There you are!' Diane stood at the doorway. She looked radiant as she had her hair done, and her face was bronzed from a sun bed.

'I thought you might be here. Marianne, you are such a stranger these days. Who is this?' Diane hovered over the table, and Marianne moved uncomfortably. Lillian smiled at Diane who positively drooled over her. Marianne introduced them; Diane was quick to take a seat, and she ordered more coffee for the table.

'These exhibitions are a little second rate, but you know sometimes you can find a little gem for the bedroom wall or for the dining room. I am always on the lookout, dear.'

Diane addressed all of her conversation to Lillian much to Marianne's annoyance, so she interjected with, 'Lillian has two paintings upstairs.' She lowered her voice and whispered, 'I think I might swap them with mine up in the Pier House; they get a better class of customer.'

'Do they?' Diane sounded surprised.

'I hear they do,' Lillian said smartly.

'Come on up and I will show them to you.'

Lillian was on her feet, and Diane followed her. Marianne sat drinking her coffee, cursing her luck. Of all the people to arrive, and she looking so well too. What was she to do now?

They were gone a good ten minutes, and when they eventually came back Lillian was quiet but Diane chatted excitedly. 'Now you see, Marianne, just like I said, you may find little gems here and there. I don't mind telling you that I am now the proud owner of two delightful paintings, so there is no need to swap with yours up in the Pier house. This little artist, who, I might add, is extremely humble, has just sold two paintings to yours truly. And not only that, she has agreed to come to my dinner party on Saturday. Not bad for a day's work, hey?' The bottom fell out of Marianne's world and she wanted to scream and say many things, but all she could do was smile and nod. Lillian sighed like she sensed that Marianne was choking inside. Marianne wanted to scream aloud that firstly the paintings were no good and they weren't worth a hundred, never mind five hundred each. Secondly if Diane wanted to buy some decent paintings there were plenty up in the Pier House, including her own. But she didn't, and she just sat there meekly whilst Diane paid for the coffee. Marianne went home alone; she left Diane with Lillian. They were having drinks in the Pier House, getting on like a house on fire. She tired listening to Diane talking nonsense about the merits of art and then Lillian agreeing with everything that she said and as the evening wore on Marianne got the unmistakable impression that they were becoming very cosy. She could see that Diane was grooming her, using her patronage as the carrot.

As she drove down to the bridge at Kilbrittain Creek she was sad, as she never did get the chance to tell Lillian how she felt. Not that it would make much difference now. Lillian was smitten, she could tell, by the lure of Diane's money, and when she went to the dinner party and saw the house and its views of the enormous farm there would be no going back then. When home she made herself tea but then she opened a bottle of Chardonnay from the fridge, and after a couple of glasses she wanted to break the glass against the wall such was her frustration. Picking up her mobile she rang Diane's house. There was no answer. Diane wasn't home yet. She thought she might ring her mobile, but then she changed her mind. Ringing the house again, she left a message for Diane to contact her. Perhaps telling on Joseph was the only weapon that she had left to use. After all, Diane was ninety-nine percent reputation and only one percent integrity. She opened another bottle of wine and she drank it too fast, and then she felt tipsy and had to lie out on the couch. She fell asleep and she dreamed that she called Joseph, and he was distant and matter of fact and he wasn't nervous at all, which unsettled her.

'You know Diane gave me your laptop?'
'Yes, I meant to thank you for that.'
'This is awkward, Joe, but there were some images. I found them by accident you know.'
'Images?'
'Yes, photographs of midgets and dwarfs engaged in all sorts of stuff. Not very pleasant, Joseph.'
Joseph was quiet for a second, and then he said,
'Midgets and dwarfs...that isn't illegal, is it?'

'No, not as far as I know, no. But I am sure you don't want people finding out.'

'Marianne, are you blackmailing me?'

'No.'

'Sounds like you are.'

'No, I just want you to know that I know, and maybe we can do each other a favour. I can stay quiet about all of that midget stuff, and you can reel her in.'

'Reel her in?'

'Yeah, she is taking what is mine. Lillian belongs to me!'

'Lillian? Who is Lillian? Say, it is not illegal. Is it? I would never have looked at that stuff if it were illegal. I didn't think it was illegal!'

'It isn't illegal. Look, best forget we ever spoke about this. Look it, Joseph, I am sorry I ever saw the stuff on your laptop. Hey, look, it's your own business. Nobody gets hurt. It certainly isn't any of my business. I just want you to know about Diane, like what she is doing. It can't be right, and you her husband.'

'Diane has her own life, Marianne, there's nothing I can do about it. That is Diane. She likes nice things, and when she sees something she likes she just goes and gets it. I am sorry about the photographs, but that's all I can say about any of this. I am sorry, really sorry.'

The dinner party was an annual event, and both Joseph and Diane went to great trouble organising caterers and gently wooing Mrs Ball to provide some of her specialities. They invited the Brogans, fellow farmers and horsey people. They lived on the other side of Kilbrittain, and the O'Briens. He was a pharmacist, and she was a retired GP. They lived in Timoleague but she was from out west originally, and he was from Bandon.

The rest were mainly friends of Diane, the arty crowd, and Sheila Walsh was there to add controversy and colour, and of course Marianne and Lillian. Maggie Ryan made her excuses even though she wasn't invited, and she let them know with a string of expletives all about how they were compromised by a benefactor that wouldn't know art if it jumped up to bite her. Joseph sat with his farm manager, a thin rat-like fellow who was less than five foot six; he sported one of those silly beards that went out from the chin like the hairs on a paintbrush. Diane was mingling, talking loudly and casting her enthusiastic spell as only she could. The great fire was lit, and the guests were drawn to it repeatedly. Marianne spoke to Mr O'Brien. He was a most affable man who she understood to know a little about almost everything, and indeed he seemed to have a fine knowledge of the arts. Earlier Sheila Walsh had shocked him by repeating her political mantra: 'There are no politics. If women are not at the coal face then politics doesn't exist. Mr O' Brien, what you are actually looking at is a kind of gender dictatorship. Is that what you would like to see?' Mr O' Brien was unused to such female rhetoric, but he tried hard to stand his ground muttering under his breath and smiling at Sheila. Greta, his wife, intervened. 'Yes, but women have to respect politics and its rules and traditions before they can just barge their way into the mire. I would have no respect for a country ruled by anarchists, even if they were women. Is that not true, Ms Walsh? We must have respect for our institutions; it is in essence all that we have.'

'No, madam,' Sheila said kindly, 'not when the institutions are male in their gestation. If all that's good and proper is male, then I say to hell with it. We need to replace it or at least add enough political water to dilute it. The more we destroy these fucking traditions, the more women will find emancipation and freedom.'

'Maybe we don't all need that kind of emancipation; maybe some of us love our men,' Greta said sharply. She linked her husband's arm and he smiled automatically, but he didn't say anything. Sheila was happy that she had made her point and had initiated the battle. She moved on down the room towards the bay window. A small group of people chatted there, and soon she was in the thick of it. Diane was in full flight reminding the O' Briens that the Brogans would be sitting next to them at the dinner table. She watched Greta closely, awaiting a reaction.

'I won't mention the poor horse.'

'No, Greta, please don't!' Mr O' Brien laughed.

'Poor Greta clipped one of their horses at the Point to Point out in Kinsale.'

'The bloody beast ran out in front of me,' Greta said. Giggling, she covered her mouth so nobody would see.

'Anyhow, the girl didn't have a tight enough hold of the poor horse.'

'What happened to the horse?' Marianne asked.

'The horse was grand.' Mr O' Brien chuckled.

'But the jeep cost three hundred euro to fix. I should have given Brogan the bill!'

'It was Brogan's horse?' Marianne said, looking around to see where Lillian was, and then eyeing her floating around the room with a glass of red wine in her hand.

'It was.' Mr O' Brien smiled. Marianne barely heard him; she was determined to say something to Lillian before the music started. If only she could get a few minutes alone with her. But every time she started to chat, Diane intervened to introduce this one and that one, or Sheila Walsh would come over spouting about politics. But she would get an opportunity. Marianne had to believe that she would get a chance to tell Lillian how she felt about her. Then she felt suddenly sad as it was almost like Lillian had sensed it from her. She had smelled her want and need; that was why she kept moving away talking to idle strangers, her facial expression so intent, like she was discussing

65

something of great importance. Diane was watching her too, for each time Marianne spied Lillian she also checked to see if Diane was watching her, and she was. Once or twice their eyes met in the crossfire.

The meal was served with Diane at the head of the table and Joseph at the opposite end. They were joint heads of the table, as it were. The starter was soup and rolls or pate and thinly sliced toast, followed by the main course, which was delicious pheasant or duck, and there was an alternative of wild darns of salmon with Mrs Ball's special sauce. The main courses were accompanied by roast potatoes and abundant vegetables, and all was washed down by expensive bottles of red and white wine and jugs of Perrier water. Marianne was grateful that Lillian was seated three down from Diane and two up from herself. Diane was busy smiling down the table at all and sundry. Lillian was quiet, concentrating on her food. She was having duck and she ate it elegantly, stopping momentarily to sip her wine. Marianne watched her. It was all so controlled and ladylike. When Lillian glanced down the table Marianne looked away as if distracted by something trivial, and when she glanced back at Lillian she was busy eating again. Diane chatted to some horsey friend of Joseph's who owned a big stud farm in the midlands. His wife had died recently and Marianne noticed that Diane was very gentle with him, occasionally touching his arm when she spoke. The greying man just nodded and spoke softly to his host. Johnston and his daughter were setting up the instruments when the desserts were served. Marianne went for the ice cream cake, which was sprinkled with chocolate, whilst Lillian chose Mrs Ball's special winter pudding. One and all said the meal was beautiful, and all the guests were full and looking forward to the music. Mr O' Brien smiled at Marianne as he made his way to the conservatory where champagne was still served and people had stepped outside smoking. Marianne glanced at Lillian, who had finished eating and was sitting back sipping her red wine.

'Do you fancy going to the conservatory before the music starts?' Lillian looked down the table at her blankly.

'How long before they start? I don't want to miss anything.'

'They will be a few minutes yet,' Diane intervened, raising her voice so as to be heard above the din.

'I will fetch you, don't worry.' She smiled.

'You are so kind,' Lillian said, pulling back her chair. Marianne was still worried by Diane, so she refused to relax.

'The Johnstons are brilliant. The old man plays the violin, and Sarah is a great singer,' Diane announced to anyone who was listening.

'I tell you, and George Brady is one of the best double bassists in Munster if not the country,' the grey haired stud farmer added. It was like he had just learned to speak aloud, though his voice was extraordinarily soft.

'Come on,' Marianne said impatiently.

'I am coming,' Lillian replied, suddenly tipsy. She followed Marianne out to the conservatory, which had a fine view sweeping over the grass banks. Even though it was dark you could still see the woods quite clearly as the garden boasted extensive lighting.

'Have some champagne, Lillian; it is so much better than red wine.'

'Speak for yourself, my darling. I prefer red wine any day.' Marianne was sorry she had said anything, but Lillian was happy to lower the glass of champagne and then pick up another.

'Must be great to be rich, to afford all of this and all of this land and cattle and horses. Must make life right easy,

Marianne. How will I ever be this rich? Did I tell you that Diane has commissioned a new painting? She wants me to paint her on Mr Archibald. I will have to take a photo, won't I? She can't very well sit up on her favourite horse for days, can she?'

'Mr Archibald is a bugger. He won't stay still, not even for a photo.'

Marianne was definite, as she was knowledgeable about horses.

'We can work something out. I hear music, I must fly!'

'Don't.' Marianne panicked.

'No, please, Lillian, please stay. Just for a minute, will you?'

'You have gone red, Marianne. Your cheeks are like beetroot.'

'I am embarrassed a little. They are just warming up. The music won't start, not for a few minutes. No, Lillian, I have been wanting to talk to you...about us.'

'Us?'

'I have feelings for you. I just want you to know that I have feelings for you and I was wondering...do you share these feelings? You know, to be honest, I am trying to tell you that I am madly in love with you.'

Marianne drank her champagne down, and in the background she heard Sarah Johnston start the first song and the music played mellow throughout the dining room, drifting slowly into the conservatory.

'I can't, Marianne,' Lillian said before darting away and back to the dining room. Marianne stood rigid, unsure of what had happened and wondering what on earth she could do next.

*

Six Years Later

The rain had eased. The pools relaxed and the gulls
mingled at last and then squabbled, and the traffic was
sparse. The evening was fortifying itself to defend against
the onslaught of night.

'You are a good dancer, Lillian. In fact I have never seen
anyone dance quite like you on that night of Diane's party.
You wore the young men out, and for a while I was sure
that I had made a huge mistake. I thought that was why you
had walked away from me. You didn't take to my advances
because young men were your fancy, but then Diane
intervened just as the music finished and the Johnstons
were playing their encore.'

'Diane was very persuasive, Marianne. Honestly, before
that night I had never engaged with a woman. It was always
men, you know?'

Marianne looked at her kindly.

'She sure was.'

'I was very drunk too; if I remember correctly, but you
know it didn't last. I mean, none of it lasted. Not me and
Diane or this whole women thing. I am married now; we
have a daughter, Isobel. I guess it wasn't for me.'

Lillian tried to distract herself; she no longer wished to
stare into Marianne's eyes so intently as she found it
unpleasant and disturbing.

'Sheila saw you out in the garden in the shadows. It was
she who told me, and it was only when I saw her so
distraught that I realised that she was so much in love with
Diane. At first I thought she was drunk, but she wasn't
drunk, Lillian, not really. She was heartbroken.'

'I think she loved Sheila, but Diane tired of everything so
easily. She used to say she loved me, but when I asked her
could I move in, Marianne, she always made an excuse and

lots of promises. But I never did move in. And then there was the tragedy—you know, when Joseph hung himself in the woods and she found him. It was really dreadful. It took everything from her.'

Marianne coughed. It was deep and growly and somehow it seemed to strangle her breath, and Lillian stood prepared to slap her on the back if needed. But Marianne, used to it, wheeled herself to the bedside locker and opening it she took out a plain card.

'I get one of these around this time every year. I think it's someone's idea of a sick joke to be honest, Lillian. I have no idea who sends them to me!' Lillian went to sit on the bed so as she could read the card over Marianne's shoulder, but Marianne held it away from her so as she couldn't see it properly.

'Let me see it; I may recognise the handwriting.' But Marianne closed it over.

'I don't want to know who is sending them. It might only give them satisfaction. No, I think this is best left.' Opening the card once more, 'It says, "Three blind mice, three blind mice, see how they run, see how they run, they all ran after the farmer's wife, she cut off their tails with a carving knife, did you ever see such a sight in your life, three blind mice!"'

'Someone's sick alright, Marianne, especially after poor Joseph killed himself. Bloody awful. Sick really!'

Marianne lifted her head from the card; tears ran through tunnels of skin, wetting her cheeks.

'She went away after that. I think she went to England. She sold the place for a song.'

'She did.' Marianne said.

'I was sort of glad she went. That was dreadful, wasn't it? I almost wished bad on her, but it's the truth, I was glad that she was gone. It really didn't matter why she left.'

'I know,' Lillian said.

'I felt the same because she just dropped me despite all of the promises and the commissions. She never gave herself to me. Once she got what she wanted from me, she just moved on. I have to be honest, I was glad she left too.'
Marianne tried to stop the tears but to no avail, and Lillian handed her a tissue from the bedside locker.
'I never heard another word.'
'Nor me, or Sheila.'
'Diane was very strange,' Lillian said.

THE SAD LADY OF LISLEE

I watch the rain fall in sheets over the fields, cleansing green. It comes from the summit of Cuckoo Hill, all rains and gullies, and my eyes are wells. I long to be there, to stand alone and let it reach me, to cleanse my soul, my sinner soul that has sent me here. Aye, for all its beauty this is a desperate place, with the wind and rain howling in my ear and the strange voices raging in my head. It is easily said that I should rage back, but it is what the gods have sent me, and all the beauty of this landscape can't change that. No, not the sound of the birds or the silent rabbit foraging, nor the crow banger or the silence when the wind stops. For I am a woman and I want to scream at this wilderness! Listen to me cry with a whimper. Each morning as you wake you hear me cry faintly, whimper. You hear me cry to you.

'I didn't know you were artistic,' Jack said, his head part hidden as he searched for the breadknife to cut the pan.
'Didn't you?' Ursula said.
'Kind of strange when I have been sending stuff to magazines these years.'
'There was me, thinkin' you were askin' for recipes and the like.'
Jack got up to go to the kitchen drawer to get the breadknife.
'It's in the sink. I washed it earlier.'
He didn't reply; he just went straight to the sink to get the knife. He wiped it with a tea towel before returning.
'She got away alright then?'
'She did, after a struggle.'
Jack started to cut the pan, but he was cutting it very thick and making crumbs so Ursula said, 'I will do it.' He capitulated, sitting back. Ursula thought that he was

looking well with his thick black head of hair. He had grown a beard that didn't suit him, because it was grey and he was black. She thought that it made him look older.

'I dunno what we are to do with her,' he said dolefully.

'She is gettin' worse. I think she is.'

'It's not like there is a cure, Jack.'

'No.'

'It doesn't get any better. Here you go.'

Ursula put three thick slices of bread on his plate, and Jack poured himself some fresh tea. He offered to fill her cup, but she shook her head.

'Nah, I will be peeing for the day.'

'It is alright now, I suppose, but how will we manage in ten years?' Jack spluttered because his mouth was full. He wiped some crumbs from his lips using his sleeve.

'We will be fucked then, Ursula.'

'Dunno,' she said calmly.

'We could always send her over to Bobby. He was the only one who could pacify her.'

'Jesus, yeah, she would love Australia. The heat and the bloody kangaroos. She freaks at the cows, so imagine her over there. She wouldn't last a minute!'

'He has a way with her, though. I wish he was still here.'

'There's nuthin' here, only this old place. These few lousy acres aren't goin' to feed him.'

'No, not with his education. Think about what he is earning down there. God, he would want to own the company over here. Do you miss him, Jack? Like, I mean besides just helping around the place. Do you actually miss him? Miss seeing him, you know, the way he laughs? And remember how he sang in the shower all of the time, and you telling him to shut up?'

'Ah, that. He could sing, mind you, it was more the songs he was singin'.'

He pulled his chair away from the table. It was akin to inserting a full stop in the conversation. He was on his feet. 'I want to go up to the creamery. I need to get some wire for the fence over by the temple.'

'Will you be long?' Ursula asked.

'They will be dropping Juliane early today.'

'Where are you goin'?'

'Nowhere.'

'I thought you were off out, no?'

'No, it is just the way she was acting up. You know, it would be easier if you were around.'

'I won't be far away.' He went out to the yard, and Ursula heard him start the jeep. She sat awhile looking at the dirty plates and saucers. The small knife was stained with butter, and the teaspoons had traces of egg. She dreaded the washing up. To spend so long standing in the one place, daydreaming mostly. It seemed such a useless way to spend time. Maybe she should put on the radio, but she dismissed that. The news was depressing and the presenters were patronising, to say the least. No, she would enjoy the quiet whilst it lasted, gathering up the plates slowly, bringing them to the sink, cursing when a teaspoon spun from a plate and on to the tiles.

'Goddamn it,' she said, but it wasn't the falling spoon that annoyed her. No, it was the sound it made. Maybe she would make some soda bread; that would be nice. But then she remembered she had loads of pan left, and they would never use it up. She rinsed the dishes. They clattered and wailed as she placed the plates standing upright in the drying rack, but invariably they fell over each time she added another, the sound grating on her nerves. When finished she went into the sitting room and up the short stairs to her bedroom. The air was cold, as Jack had turned off the boiler before breakfast. Ursula decided to check her e-mails before getting dressed. She thought of a shower, but she had run off the hot water with the dishes so she decided that she would have one later as she wasn't going anywhere. The e-mails were bland. There were two from Bobby. Nothing much. She laughed to herself as no matter how she tried she persisted on reading his mails with an Aussie twang.

Everything was

"G'day, mate,"

"Hww's Sheila,"

"C'mon, Skip."

Bobby was telling her about his girlfriend. Her name was Claire, and she was from Dublin. God, Ursula thought, *he goes all the way to Perth to meet a lassie from Dublin.* Well, there you go now. She was much older than him, like three years. *Does he know that his father was seven years older than his mother? Now that is old.* The job was grand with a chance of promotion; well, he hoped so anyway. Just keeping the powder dry, head down, that sort of thing, and he was moving flat soon as the other guys were moving on. Two were going to New Zealand, and one had enough and he was heading home. Bobby was thinking of moving in with an English guy that he worked with, but Claire had room in her place so maybe he might go there. "Maybe." *Maybe ya think I came down in the last shower.* The other e-mail from Bobby was a joke thing on Ireland and Enda Kenny with a wig that made him look like Margaret Thatcher, hee hee hee! Ok, now Facebook or Twitter. Twitter, as Evelyn Connolly was always on Facebook, and she didn't fancy engaging with her this early in the day. Twitter was quiet. Ursula checked under notifications; there was nothing new. She clicked on her Twitter profile, @ursulautism, and her followers and the following stats appeared: she followed 545 and was followed by 132. Something wrong here, she thought. I obviously don't appeal to the masses, but then who cares about autism anyhow? She relaxed a little as she composed a tweet.

'My daughter had a difficult morning, but eventually she calmed down. I wait for her return not knowing!'

She read over it twice before sending, and then she admonished herself, as people would think she was selfish and only concerned about herself. A minute later her tweet was favoured by @Davidmorgan. She also received a reply.

'The mornings were always the worst with my son James. Like you, I would never know what to expect!'#autism

Ursula replied, 'People don't understand, the moods are so unpredictable!'#autism.

She left the PC momentarily to gather her clothes for the day. She wanted to go casual with jeans and her boots. She liked the pure wool sweater that Evelyn bought her for her birthday. She laid them all out neatly, returning to the PC.

'I no longer live with James, but I am sure all is still the same. When I go see him he doesn't know me!'

Ursula read it over a few times to make sure that she was reading it correctly then she typed, 'I am sorry for you. It is hard to live with & impossible to live without!'

She waited for a minute but there was no reply, save for in her notifications. It said, 'David Morgan is now following you, @Davidmorgan.' She clicked. Following 2,057; followers, 2,796. Wow, he is popular. She saw he had a link to a webpage, so she clicked on that. David Morgan, Literary Agent, Cork. It went on to list the books and writers that he represented. Ursula knew most of them; they weren't the crème de la crème, but they were fairly well known. There was a photograph also. He was tall with fair hair. She put him at around fifty. He looked dishy in his suit. She wondered: would he help her with her work? Could he help her get published? Maybe, but he was a great new follower on Twitter.

77

I sometimes dream of the sea. It churns its way through the valley, filling nooks, then crannies. I dream of dark places where memories live and time stands still. I want to return and ask all of the questions that I should have asked, but, hey, I need the answers now. In truth I need to know the world's opinion of me. Am I a good person? Am I not? The thoughts lead me beyond the valley to the dark place. The wash lashes the rocks right in front of me, and I am the only witness to this storm. Ten feet away the world rages, and then silence. I recede to Mother. She sees me perfect, yet I am not. I have become years old now, and for a split second she has empathy. I know by her eyes and the water levels rising. She screams again, and I am awake. The gods are pleased with visceral blood. The animals sink in the mud, and the dead mules scratch their behinds off the iron gates and the dogs bark in the distance. On one wet day she accuses me of arrogance, that arrogance that stands in the cold fields. Then she screams at me as I am woman, giver of life. But I have failed, for what I would give is trapped without air in a jar. She spits on the green and condemns it to wallpaper. She wants to know why I am not a PC. I have no answers now just because the questions were never asked.

'She is quiet,' Jack said.
'I will have to go get wire in the mornin'.
It was ordered, but it hasn't come yet.'
He was turning on the heat.
'That dog is a nuisance, Ursula. She is due any day. More trouble on the way.'
'Evelyn will take one.'
'She says that, but when it comes to it…,' Jack said.
'We will find good homes.'
'We may drown half of them.'

78

He was gone out to the yard. *There will be no drowning.*
She peered through the dividing doors; satisfied, she went
to the fridge to get the mince. Spaghetti Bolognese, her
favourite, but she had to do lamb chops for Jack as he hated
Bolognese. He called it women's food. She went to the
sink, and through the window Jack was bringing food into
the shed for Elsie. The springer's face appeared at the door.
She acknowledged her owner with a yelp and a quick turn.
Jack disappeared into the darkness. The evening was
closing in, and he turned on the light in the outhouse. She
had better go and check on Juliane again. She wasn't to be
left in front of the television for too long. Ursula watched
the late evening clouds gather at the top of the hill. They
came from the sea and some were moist; she could tell by
the light patches of grey decaying their ends.

Later as she pottered around in her room, she heard Jack
move around downstairs. He had got Juliane to bed. Maybe
she would sleep, maybe not. The medication worked, and
then it didn't. Sometimes the nights were endless, Ursula
usually taking the long shift as Jack had an early start with
the cows. She turned on the PC. No e-mails, save for one
from a cheap travel site. Travel. If only. She had one new
notification on Twitter. It was from @DavidMorgan, and
he sent her a link to a site that accepted short stories. Ursula
investigated and found an American website that published
short stories and poems. She checked the submission
guidelines and bookmarked the details.
'Thanks, David, I checked this out. Sounds great!' There
was no reply so she went into Word and continued on the
story she was working on, looking at the title:
"The Sad Lady of Lislee."
She knew that everyone would think it was all about her.
They would think she was screaming about her own life,
her own sadness at having an eighteen-year-old non-verbal

autistic daughter. Yes, they would see it as a confession, as
her coming out to shed her tears publically. Maybe she
should change it, bring it away from herself. But then she
reasoned, Sure, the story isn't about me at all or about
Juliane. No, this story is about Anne, the rector's daughter,
and how he locked her away in the tower at Lislee Temple.
He hid her away so she couldn't marry Robert Barry, the
farrier's son, who had taken a great shine to her beauty. Her
beauty was one thing, but the rector knew her mind was
slow, as she had never properly integrated with the world
from childhood. So he locked her away in the tower to
protect her from the world. And from inside her prison she
gazed over the valley of Lislee and watched the sun light
the countryside and then the darkness fall to send all to
sleep. But in between she was plotting her escape. Yes, she
liked this story, especially as it wasn't about Ursula or
Juliane. No, she had transported herself out of the narrative
completely. She received a new tweet from
@DavidMorgan.
'I sent you a Dm.'
She replied, 'Ok, will look!' Her direct message said,
'davidmorgan@live.ie Send me something, saw your photo
in Bandon Opinion, you look very well!'
Ursula replied, 'Thank you, didn't know you read the
Opinion. Ursulautism@eircom.net'
She returned to her story, concentrating on how the rector's
daughter might act when he came to visit her. But another
tweet came from David.
'My secretary is from Bandon, send me a few pages.'
'Alright, I will.'
Ursula pasted the first three pages into the body of an e-
mail, prefacing it with, 'I haven't edited this, so excuse
typos etc. Honest opinions please, thick-skinned here.
Thanks very much for your interest, David. The photo was

at the autism charity event we did in the Fernhill Hotel last
month.'

She felt a sudden rush of excitement, as nobody had
expressed any interest in her work before, and even though
he hadn't seen her work it was so exciting to be so close
and compatible with an agent. Ursula wanted to run
downstairs and tell Jack but she decided not to, as he was
most likely engrossed in some television show. He took no
interest in her writing anyhow, and he would hardly know
what a literary agent was.

*It is the only track, the only one left open to me. I have
worn it with my feet, and I have planted all the wildflowers
that make it yellow. At first I thought maybe blue or purple,
but, no, yellow is best. I see it yellow as to me the world is
made of oil paints. It is where I spring to hide, little path,
my furrow filled with sods of damp earth and minor
mountains. The little turrets are deep valleys; at least they
would be to a little spider. Sometimes I imagine the fields to
be full of apple trees, the type of thing a young girl yearns
for. Walk through in summer frock, the sun burning and the
wind browning, soft sheen on blonde, the sun piercing my
youthful skin, apples falling on their own, buckets of them. I
live in the valley of Lislee, and nearby the temple stands. It
casts a dark shadow, and it in turn seeks the protection of
dark trees. Yes, it chose evergreens, big sturdy evergreens
that are bland, and never think, and when my grandfather
was buried in the graveyard alongside I heard the grave
digger whisper that he had died with his eyes open, and I
wondered why he died, and then I wondered why he died
with his eyes open, and if he did then why did the
gravedigger whisper it. Through my internal tears I looked
over the wall and to the greenness of the valley for comfort.
I was looking for life midst the dreadful finality of death. It*

*was here I first saw the sun; it blazed along my path, and
as it did it created time.*

David Morgan was even better looking in real life, and he
was actually taller than she had expected.

'This is Sharon,' he said, introducing his secretary. She
beamed at Ursula like she had known her all of her life.

'Hello,' Ursula said, offering her hand. Sharon shook it
generously. David was very relaxed. Ursula liked that, as it
helped her stay calm.

'I was at a coffee morning in the Imperial, we did very
well,' she said.

David shuffled her through to the inner office. It was small
but compact.

'Great cause,' he said, and then he added, 'The more
money the better, Ursula, but money might not cure it.' He
went on. 'Research is the key, though, isn't it, and research
costs money.'

David relaxing, leaned back in his swivel chair.

'I would offer you a coffee, but we aint got none. Maybe
we can go over to the English Market for lunch.'

'I am coffee'ed out of it, but lunch sounds nice.' Ursula
watched him look something up on his laptop. She felt that
she should stay quiet whilst he did, but then he said, 'The
Bandon Opinion doesn't do you justice. You are far better
looking in real life. See, look.'

He turned his laptop around.

'That's James. I used to have a photo of him on my desk,
but they grow so fast. I must get a copy of this one. I am
sure Cindy will send me one.'

The boy was perfect and handsome, a real ten-year-old with
cheeky eyes.

'I hope to get over to see him at Easter.'

'Where is he?' Ursula asked.

'God, he is so handsome.'

'Cindy lives in Chester, but she is from London originally. Her new partner is from Chester.'

'I hear Chester is nice.'

'It is. I was nearly moving there, but business is business, I suppose. All my clients live here; I read your stuff by the way.'

'Oh,' Ursula said, feeling a flush.

'I need to do a lot of work on it.'

'No, not at all. On the contrary I thought it was very good. Alright, we could tidy up a few lines here and there, but I know excellent editors. Nah, it was very good. I am going to send it off to a few publishers in Dublin, but first I will have an editor look at it.'

'Ah, no, David, that would be too expensive.'

'I am owed stacks of favours, Ursula.'

'Really? I will pay for the editor, I insist.'

'Have you written much more of this Lislee story?'

Ursula laughed.

'Tons more, but I deleted it and started again. I have ten thousand words.'

'Great, we can chat about it over lunch. How about you send me the rest of it when you get home?'

David was on his feet, and he held the door open.

'We are off to lunch. If Dan O'Brien calls, put him through. Put everyone else off, alright?' Sharon smiled. Her face radiated warmth across the room, so much so that Ursula suddenly felt a little hot. Maybe it was because she was about to have lunch with an agent. Not just any agent either, as David represented Dan O'Brien, one of Ireland's most famous fiction writers, and he was renowned around the globe.

The restaurant in the English Market was busy, but after a few minutes the young waitress dressed in black found them a small table along the wall. David had already sourced and paid for their food, which he brought down on a tray. Ursula just had a ham salad sandwich and a cup of tea, whilst David had a chicken wrap and a cappuccino.

'Busy here,' Ursula said.

'Mad this time of day. So tell me, how's it in Lislee?'

'Do you know it?'

'Not really. I know Clonakilty, and I think I was in that place, The Pink Elephant, once years ago. I was meeting this client—well, he was potentially a client. The guy could write beautifully, like the real deal. But he couldn't do dialogue, which sort of killed it for me. Pity that.'

'So you didn't represent him then?'

'Nah. He was a pompous old bollix anyhow.' David took a large bite of his chicken wrap, and Ursula took the opportunity to swallow some tea.

'You're naturally blonde, I can tell. Is your daughter blonde?'

She liked the way he asked her the question; he had an innocent way of saying things.

'She is the perfect blonde, David, and very beautiful with it. To be honest if she walked in here now heads would turn.'

'Wow,' he said, and then he studied Ursula to check in case he had inadvertently caused offence.

'It is of little consolation to her,' Ursula said sadly.

'She doesn't have an image of herself, not in that sense anyhow.'

'I see,' David said.

'Your son is in Australia like the rest of them, hey?'

'Yeah, Bob's in Perth. He is doing well, but we miss him dreadfully. But what is there here? There are no jobs. Well, not good jobs. Like, we don't have any indigenous industry—well, not in sufficient quantities—and our little farm is barely viable, so off he went.'

'Hard times, Ursula.'

David was eating the last of his chicken, small pieces had fallen from the wrap and somehow had landed on his plate. 'Juliane goes to respite three days a week, but we had to fight to keep her on it once she turned eighteen. When you have a disabled child in this country, David, you have to fight for everything. It's like people don't really care once they and their loved ones are well. People think it's someone else's responsibility. I don't know what things are like in England, but they're shit here.'

'I dunno about the UK. Cindy looks after all of that. She doesn't complain much, so it must be ok.'

'Forgive me, David,' Ursula said.

'I am campaigning too long, and now I have gone sour.'

'Not at all. You are dead right, people just don't see it.'

'Tell me about your business. How do you deal with all of those famous writers and their egos?' David wiped the grease from his fingers with a paper napkin. He looked directly into her eyes, and she saw how deep and brown his eyes actually were.

'Just like I talk to you. I let them rant on, and I just stay as I am. Like, some of them don't take criticism so well, especially when you remind them of their limitations. Writers don't do limitations Ursula, they are so insecure that any notion of control freaks them out. Honestly, it's like this forgive the analogy, but they all want to drown in their own shit. Even though they know that they could get out of it if they opened their minds and listened just for once. And if by some miracle they do, well, then I get the thank you calls when the fat royalty cheque arrives!'

He finished his cappuccino like it was some kind of a reward for his speech. When she left him she was sad that he was gone. It was like all the excitement had suddenly exited her life. She went pottering around the English Market in an attempt to distract herself, but all she did was bump into people and she soon tired of apologising. Her inner voice screamed to go buy fish; such were the delights in the fish mongers. But then she worried about the heat in the car on the way home, and buying a bag of ice was all too complicated. So in the end she left without buying anything at all. The world was busy out on Grand Parade, and the traffic was endless coming round the corner from Washington Street. Her car was on level three of the Grand Parade car park, and the tariff was very expensive. Once settled she caught a glimpse of herself in the driver's mirror, and she convinced herself that she was still attractive for her age. She had none of the ailments one associates with women of her age. No afflictions like facial hair or sagging beneath the eyes. Maybe David liked her more than her book. She felt guilty at the thought, as her car screeched down to the next level. It wasn't anything that he said as such. It was more in the way that he looked at her and then looked away sharply if she eyed him back inquisitively. Anyway she was sure that she imagined it all, and her car stopped screeching when she reached the street.

Juliane had kicked up. When she arrived home Jack was still in a mood over it. He was quiet over his dinner and he went out straight after it, and he didn't say where he was going and Ursula didn't ask. Juliane was lying on the sofa covered with a blanket; that was how he left her. Ursula watched her from the kitchen through the dividing doors; she was thinking of her work and how she was going to e-mail David more of her story later and how exciting all of this was. But it was so hard to enjoy her success. It was nigh impossible to feel elated just to see her daughter lie drowsily on the sofa, knowing that her husband had reached the end of his patience with her. For a moment Ursula tried to imagine her as a sick child, that all of this was only temporary. Later Juliane would feel better. The illness would pass, and she would be back on her feet just like a normal girl. She was suddenly guilty about her romantic ramblings too. This was her real world; any thoughts of being a well-known author with a handsome agent were futile. What would a man like David Morgan want with her anyhow? No doubt he would have loads of prospective clients younger and far prettier than she and with no baggage too. Later when Jack came back she went to her room. The computer looked lonely, the screen dark. It seemed to smile when she turned it on. She read through her story and when she reached the point at which she had stopped she was disappointed, partly because the story ended abruptly but also because she would have liked to send him the piece where the rector goes to see his daughter, who is locked in the tower. But the mood wasn't right to continue. It could take hours just to write five hundred words, and Jack might need a hand to get Juliane to bed. She listened to see if there was any inkling of sound from downstairs, but there wasn't. All was quiet. Ursula started to type, describing the rector as robust and red-faced, his breathing heavy as he climbed the spiral staircase to the room where Anne was incarcerated. The room was lit by the angled light spearing through the narrow windows, but the morning was dark so at first he didn't see her sitting in the corner. When he got nearer she bowed her head away from him. He went to speak but she looked up suddenly, and although she was his own flesh and blood he was struck by her beauty, and even in the dull light her eyes piercing blue penetrated him and shook his heart. The rector trembled and took a step back.

Ursula stopped writing for a second. Jack was putting Juliane to bed. She could hear the toilet flushing downstairs and then she heard Jack's voice, a faint reassuring mumble. Continuing with her writing, Ursula began typing. The rector reached out to touch Anne's face but just as his fingertips reached the softness of her cheek, she withdrew from him, she sprang to her feet and rushed past him to cower in the far corner, burying her head in her chest. All he could see was her long blonde hair swishing the floor like a broom.

'I am doing this for you, my love, to keep you safe. That Robert Barry has bad intentions, my love. He is driven by the greed of his loins. He has no interest in your condition. Why, as soon as he has his way he will cast you aside, unwanted and maybe with child.'

Anne kept rocking her head. Her sweeping made the dust rise, and the rector could see it dancing within the pillars of light.

'I know you have not got a sound mind, my love, but don't you see that you are the Lady of Lislee. Everything that you see from here is yours. All the fields, the trees, this valley belongs to you. I have gifted it to you in my will.'

The rector sighed as his daughter stayed with her head down. His words were lost, and he wondered why he had bothered to utter them at all. The mobile rang and Ursula said, 'Hi, Eve. Nah, I am messing around with this story I'm working on. What? No, I don't have an agent, not yet. No, I didn't, I said that he was interested, but there is nothing concrete not yet. These things take time. 'What? Yeah, I did. In the English Market. He paid. I just had a sandwich. It was packed. No, it is just him and his secretary. Yeah, her name is Sharon. She was nice, very smiley. Hah, you know me now and smiley people. Ah, we will see. I don't have my hopes up. The market is full of historical fiction; one more won't set the world alight. 'She is alright; quiet now, but Jack was stressed earlier. Nah, just the usual. She is off tomorrow. They don't take her on Fridays anymore. Cutbacks, you know. 'In Clonakilty. No, they closed that. It's gone now altogether. Not tomorrow, Eve, no. I think I will take her for a walk if it's nice in the afternoon. We might go up to Coolim. What? I will not, although sometimes I feel like it. Maybe Saturday. How are you Saturday? But not for long. I usually go to Supervalu. Dunne's are handy alright. I just find Supervalu nearer, but whatever. We will have a coffee. Right. Ok, I will see you then. Bye bye!' Ursula checked her e-mail messages; both the phone call and this legitimate distraction replaced the intensity of writing. There was one new message from David Morgan.

'Hi, Ursula, enjoyed meeting you. Pity we didn't have more time to chat, but don't forget to send me on the rest of your work. Hope we can chat again soon. David.'

She read it again and then once more, and it wasn't that it was long or in any way intricate, but somehow she took pleasure over reading his words. She even managed to match his voice to it, her mind playing tricks as she read with his voice having more gravitas each time. Then she laughed as she over-emphasised words like "chat again soon." Jack walked into the bedroom; he looked at the computer mournfully.

'She is down. I am going over to Holland's for a pint with Teddy Burke. He is callin' in a few minutes. Do you have any cash? I forget to go to the ATM.'

'You forgot?' Ursula said, reaching for her bag.

'I only have a fifty.

'Wait, I might have a few twenties in the zip.' And she had because she had paid the car park in Grand Parade with a fifty, and that was the change.

'What are you up to?' Jack said, changing his sweater.

'Finishing off some of my story. Well, it's not finished, but this agent wants it.'

'Agent? That sounds posh.'

'With my luck it will come to nothing, Jack.'

'You never know, Ursula, you could end up like Maeve Binchy. She made a stack.'

'She did, but I doubt if I will even get published. I met the
agent today in Cork. He was nice, but sort of vague, you
know?'
'I thought you were in the Imperial.'
'I was, but I met him for lunch.'
'Good on you. There he is. Listen, I won't be late.'
Jack was gone, and she could hear the boring tat tat tat of
Teddy Burke's jeep ticking over in the yard.

*In the end the miracle is that we are alive at all just
because each one of us is weak and fragile. I know because
I watch the patterns in the wind, and sometimes it is such
that it blows right through me. I can feel it fanning my
bones. Oh, wind that dries the saps of trees, that combs the
meadow grass. I stare at you, all-perfect ghost flutterer,
silent stranger tramples the grass. Did I ever see the little
girl there? The one who allowed the sun turn her bronze or
the child who wanders aimlessly, aimlessly picking at
straw, looking skyward then downward and finally
wayward. Did I ever see her love the gentle roll of land all
the way along to Coolbawn? These Everest hills are full of
black and white dairy cows. They are the still ones, but the
child knows they have a ticket with their name on it. Look,
it is there, stuck in their ears. What child wants to bang
their behinds with a fragile stick? Then excuse them for
having their rear ends destroyed with excrement. What
value time as the child washes her face in the streams that
flow down the gullies of Cuckoo Hill? To her the rivers are
damned, and all sweat is useless.*

'Tell me, what is he like? Come on, Ursula, don't be shy.'
Evelyn was reaching into her pocket to pay but Ursula beat
her to it and the waitress smiled and said thanks, so Evelyn
said once again,
'Well?'

Ursula smiled at her across the small table.

'He is very handsome. A little younger than you, Evelyn, but very self-assured.'

'Like I am not?'

Evelyn pretended to be hurt.

'Is he going to get you a book deal?' Her voice was laced with excitement.

'I doubt it, but he is interested. Like, he wanted to see more of my stuff, so that's good.'

Ursula was wiping her plate with a napkin.

'That is good,' Evelyn said graciously. She drank some coffee and then went on.

'Maybe he will get you a huge deal like Cecilia Ahern, hey?' Ursula, getting embarrassed, said, 'I wouldn't mind her money, but I dunno if I want to write like her.'

They both laughed. Evelyn removed her glasses to clean them so as she could see Ursula better, but when she did Ursula noticed how pale she was.

'Are you getting enough sleep, my dear? You look so pale.'

Evelyn was five years younger but didn't always look it. She had fallen victim to menopause and didn't exactly put up a brave fight. Thus she was overweight with a lazy posture. She wore thick glasses, and worst of all her unwanted facial hair conspired to age her dreadfully.

'If I sleep anymore, I will be certified as dead.' Evelyn spat at her own joke, drops of coffee flooding her saucer. Ursula looked away and pretended not to notice.

'You know the painting you have hanging in the hall?'

Evelyn looked at Ursula, surprised that she had brought up her mother's painting.

'It isn't worth anything. Mammy said it was worthless. She got it from a maiden aunt. She was daft, mind you. A good old Belfast wimman.'

'No, I don't care what it is worth,' Ursula said curtly.

'Juliane loves it. She always stops and looks at it, and she

91

makes to go out into the hall anytime we are in your living room. I used to think it was the gull just floating in the wind and the high seas storming around it, but I don't think so now. I think she is fascinated by the isolation. The gull is so alone.' Evelyn wasn't sure of what to say so she just blurted, 'Whatever you are into, Ursula.'

Ursula thanked the waitress for the receipt, and the waitress smiled.

'I am sure it is,' Ursula said.

'You are getting very arty. It's all of this hanging round with agents and the like. I think I might have lost my friend.' Ursula laughed at Evelyn's serious face.

'You should never judge a book by its cover, my dear,' Ursula said light-heartedly, getting up. The waitress thanked her for the tip.

'You are very generous all of a sudden.' Evelyn squeezed herself out of the narrow seat.

'She was good,' Ursula said, loud enough for the girl to hear her.

'Very good.'

And out they went into the rain, and Evelyn said, 'Where are you parked?'

'I am miles away at the church.' Ursula was looking at the rain. It got heavier as she spoke; she stepped back into a shop doorway for shelter.

'I will run you up,' Evelyn said, raising her voice as the rain lashed down.

'I am just down here.' They made a run for it and soon sat soaked in the Volkswagen golf. Ursula got that damp smell from her clothes, and Evelyn wiped the windshield feverishly so as she could see.

'You can have that painting if you like,' she said generously.

'It is worth nothing. I actually did get Michael Plaice to look at it.'

'Did you now. Thanks very much. I might take you up on that yet.'

Evelyn glanced at her friend, trying to decipher her mood. 'If Juliane likes it, you can have it,' she said, turning the car, the rain slushing down the windscreen. She turned the wipers on to full, and Ursula leaned forward so she could see where they were going.

'Michael Plaice would know alright. There is nothing he doesn't know about these things. Hey, what was he doing over in your place anyhow?' Evelyn went red, but she was too busy looking at the road to betray herself fully.

'I asked him to look at some of Mammy's old paintings and stuff; it was a few years ago, like.'

'You kept that quiet.'

'It was well after his divorce.'

'So what happened?'

'Nothing. He just told me the painting with the gull wasn't worth anything.'

*

From the window of the hotel she could see the small boats. They were still, and the only activity was the wind blowing through the exotic trees over by the wall. David was late, so she ordered another spring water. The barman put lemon in again, this after she had actually asked him not to. But he was polite and attentive, so she said nothing. It was a worry lately how she was suddenly taking such an interest in waiting staff, and for the life of her she couldn't figure out why it should be. She saw him come in. He wasn't in a suit. This time he wore a dark leather jacket with smart slacks. He had omitted a tie, and he had left his shirt open at the collar.

'I was delayed in Innishannon. Is there anythin' can be done about that place? Drink, go on. I am going to have one. Just one, mind.'

'I will have a red wine then,' Ursula said. She watched him go to the bar, and the barman gave him a lecture on the red wines. Surprisingly David had a pint of Guinness when she would have put him down for a shorts man.

'The Courtmac Hotel. Couldn't have picked a better joint. The view is marvellous. Does that road from Timoleague flood at high tide?'

'Sometimes, but only in places. But we often have to detour up and around through Barryroe.'

'Sounds adventurous.'

David smiled at her benignly like he was happy to be here and in her company.

'I have a publisher interested. Now, he is only small, like a one-man job, but he is very interested and very well connected. He is ex–RTE, and he has pals in the Indo and the Irish Times. He is in Dun Laoghaire. Well, his office is in Dun Laoghaire, but he lives in one of these big gaffs in Dalkey down by Coliemore harbour.

'To be honest, Ursula, I don't like the man, but it's business, you know. He is the type of fella that could set up a huge publishing house in the morning. He has it all, but you hear of self-publishing? Well, this fella is a sort of independent publisher. I think he is only in it for the wife. Mind, that's wife number three. She is from Venezuela, a real beauty. She wrote a memoir about growing up in poverty, like in the slums, and he is publishing it for her. That is how he got into publishing in the first place.' David rested for a moment; then, gulping his pint he stopped, suddenly remembering his company. He put his pint down. Ursula liked the residue it left on his lips, and he licked it off self-consciously.

'Who is he?' Ursula asked trying to sound casual.

'Alan Hardy.'

'I remember him. He was on that thing. Dragons Den.'

'Yeah, he is a real dinger. Don't know what he will offer us; he never says. We will have to meet him to discuss things. So when are you available to go to Dublin?'
'Dublin? I am not sure, David. With Juliane, Jack won't be able to cope.'
Sensing her genuine worry David said, 'Dunno, maybe he might come to Cork. I have a few more things he might have an interest in. Leave it with me, and I will see. But he is a stickler.'
'I will talk to Jack,' Ursula said sipping her wine. Boy, was she grateful for it now!

The world where cattle wade through soft water—it is what I see as we climb the mighty road up Cuckoo Hill and beyond, and I know that when we reach the top the world opens and you can see for miles, and the cattle wade by— and I am frightened of them and their bulk, and when I come to you my eyes are a soft blue. You had shown me pictures earlier of cows and fields, and I was quite excited about it all. It was then I remembered how I loved the painting of the lonely gull, and it was then that I wondered why. It was you who taught me about time. I have to admit, I had no idea about time till you pointed it out to me as we walked over the fields to Coolim Cliffs. You settled a little in front of me, and I knew that in a year's time we would barely remember this day. I wondered why it was that days slipped innocently by into memory, yet whilst we live it all is vital. I knew all about this but not many do; they trundle on aggressively like this will last forever. When you held me I struggled, but you kept a tight grip save that I should slip and fall over and miles down to the sea. You raised your head to the wind and it blow-dried your hair, and over the bay the sun broke through and warmed us momentarily.

95

*

His car was new and sporty. Ursula wondered how much it had cost. It looked so expensive.

'I lease a new car every three years,' David said. He wore sunglasses when he drove. He said it was to deflect the light, but Ursula thought them to be more of a fashion accessory. Entering Dublin he took the M50 southbound. Ursula hadn't been in Dublin for years. It had changed so much. The motorway split its way through the landscape, and much of what had been rural was now urban. The traffic moved well along three lanes. After twenty minutes they exited at Cherrywood, and David brought her on the scenic route by Killiney. 'Lovely beach. And the Dart— God, I think I was only on the Dart once in my life.'

'You don't need it where you live,' David said, smiling.

'Bono lives in there.'

'Which one?'

'That one.' He pointed with his finger.

'Very nice,' Ursula said, thoroughly enjoying herself.

'Thanks for bringing me this way; very interesting.' David chuckled and steered the car onto the Vico Road and along by the foot of Killiney Hill and then passed the beach at White Rock.

'Wow, this is beautiful,' Ursula said, taking in the view of Killiney Bay and Dalkey Island.

'Does anyone live out there?'

'No, it just gets day trippers.'

David steered the car right and around by Sorrento. The island seemed so close from this angle. He found parking in view of Coliemore Harbour. It was small with a few rowing boats moored and a fellow fishing at the end. He looked disinterested, like he had just figured the whole thing was a waste of time.

Alan Hardy's house was elevated. It had a view over the sea, and when his daughter invited them in Ursula could smell fresh flowers. The daughter was in her early twenties. She had been taught to be polite, but Ursula sensed that she could be a handful too. There was somethin' in the way she held a serious expression whilst she spoke. She showed them into the lounge and invited them to sit. Ursula chose a leather armchair whilst David sat on a hard chair by the window. He pretended to look out like there was something interesting going on outside, but there wasn't so then he said, 'Nice place.'

'Lovely,' Ursula replied and then whispered,

'I love the carpet. Very expensive.'

Alan Hardy wasn't nearly as imposing as the television made him out. He was quite small with a robust frame, and his belly hung over the belt of his trousers. He was growing a beard too, which made Ursula look at him twice to see if it was the right person. The beard didn't suit him, because he was balding on top. She thought balding men shouldn't do beards as it aged them dreadfully.

'David, you made good time.'

'This is Ursula, Alan, the lady I was telling you about.'

'He never said that you were so good looking now.'

'I don't think he likes to exaggerate. David has more sense.'

'Nonsense, my dear. He is one of the biggest spoofers in the business; always has been. What is it they say? Oh, yes, that he sold a book called "Lost at Sea" and it turned out to be about a fellow out fishing who snagged his line. That's David for you.' Ursula looked at David to see how he was taking it all, but he just sat smiling like the whole banter amused him.

'You have a lovely home, Alan,' Ursula said, trying to even things out.

'Yes, I bought this before the boom, and it rocketed, I can tell you. God, yer man, the racing car fellow—can't think of his name—he offered me two million for it. I turned him down. And yer woman, Cantwell, the opera singer, she wanted it too, but she didn't want to pay for it, so I told her to fuck off. Then the recession hit, and I wouldn't get a million for it now. I doubt it. Seven-fifty maybe.'

The daughter then arrived with a tray with tea and biscuits. Her father stared at her like he had just seen her for the first time. She smiled as she placed the tray on the coffee table, and when she turned to leave Ursula noticed that she had a perfect figure.

Alan watched her till she left the room.

'That's Jean. She is super intelligent. She is doing a degree in English literature, and the tutors are in awe of her.'

'Where is she doing it?' David asked.

'Trinity,' Alan said like it was a really stupid question.

'It is handy, because she critiques the manuscripts for me. Sure, what clue would I have? I am a businessman, not an arty farty. She liked your work, though.'

Alan looked at David rather than Ursula, which made her nervous, but then David said, 'So what do you have in mind then?' Alan looked at him incredulously, but then with a modicum of decency he acknowledged Ursula's discomfort by smiling.

'Nothing much, David. You know the industry better than me. A new name, an unknown. Yes, talented, we will allow that, but it's a huge risk for us. Normally we do advances, maybe up to ten grand but with something new like this we couldn't entertain an advance, to be honest. But we are willing to buy it when it is finished. That's if we still like it, mind.' Ursula watched as David changed from the banal to the serious.

'We would always look for a small advance, Alan, you know that, but what would you give us for the completed book?' Alan reached for his tea. Ursula was sure that it had gone cold as he hadn't touched it, and David in some sort of subliminal response put his cup and saucer back on the tray.

'Jean wasn't all that mad about it, David. She liked it overall, but there was lots wrong with it, my dear. Grammar and plot. Jean didn't think it made any sense, dear. She proposed loads of changes. I will go and get the file.'

He was up, and he shuffled out of the room like he had just remembered that he had some affliction. David, looking at Ursula, threw his eyes to heaven.

'This is typical of him. He is just trying to be all hard arse business-like, but he wants to buy it; I know that, so just bear with it.'

Ursula just wanted it to end. There was something dreadful about people discussing her work in these terms. She had worked so hard to put it all together. Then she chided herself for allowing things to get personal—but then the book was so personal. Maybe that was the problem. Alan returned with the file. He shuffled back to his seat, almost sitting on the cup and saucer he had left resting there. David pointed to it, and Alan looked around over-dramatically before finally lifting it and placing it on the tray. He opened his file and pretended to engage with its contents. After a minute he looked up and, peering first at Ursula and then David, he said, 'We will buy it for ten grand. We can advance you two if you really need it.'

Ursula, fed up of being subservient, said, 'what do you propose to do with it then, Mr, Hardy?' Alan looked at David, and David responded, 'They will market it and get it reviewed.'

'All over the planet. The Hardy imprint is known everywhere now. It will be reviewed in London, New York, Beijing. We will place adverts in the press and in arts magazines and the like,' Alan said.

'I dunno,' Ursula said.

'It's not the money—don't get me wrong, I am not worried about the money as such. It's more about my personal life. My daughter, Juliane, is autistic, and this is personal to me. I wonder, should I wait and finish the book before considering any offers?'

David thought for a second before saying, 'Of course, you are right. We don't have to rush into anything now. We can always pitch it when it is finished. If we were to give over the rights now, sure, we might live to regret it.'

'You won't get a better offer here in Dublin,' Alan said closing the file.

*

David was quiet on the way home, and it got dark just south of Portlaoise. He was to drop Ursula back to Kent station where she had left her car. They had stopped at a roadside service station just outside Monasterevin. He had a full dinner, which he ate self-consciously, whilst she just had a sandwich and a coffee. She didn't feel like food, and then she sensed that he was studying her.

'This is a shit business, Ursula, and fair play; you gave Hardy plenty to think about. And you were right. Fuck him and his derisory offer. We can get way more down the line.'

'The money doesn't interest me. Honest, David, it doesn't at all, save for it might help Juliane. But to think that people can be so hard, so unemotional, literally unmovable, the fact that my main character had autism didn't register…it is really strange.'

'Strange? It isn't strange, Ursula. People like Hardy don't do sentiment. He bought himself a wife, his Venezuelan slave. That was after his second wife died of agonising skin cancer, the dirt bird!'

Ursula watched the darkness fold over the motorway. The traffic coming from Cork was sparse, and every so often

100

the giant beams of headlights lit the far side of the road.
David pulled over in to a layby just north of Fermoy.
'I need to take a leak.'
When he got out a blast of cold air hit her face. It was a
reminder that summer was still distant. When he returned
the cold air blasted away once again, and he fumbled with
his safety belt.
'Do you mind if I say something to you?'
Ursula looked over, and his handsome face was lit by a
oncoming headlight, but then the darkness returned and she
could barely see him at all.
'What?'
'I just want you to know how attractive you are. I find you
very attractive, you know.'
'Ah, David, I am flattered but very married.'
'I know that. That's not important, is it? There is just the
two of us here. Just you and me, hey.'
She felt his fingers tickle the back of her neck, and then he
settled the palm of his hand around her shoulder.
'I can't do this. We had better go on.'
'Hey, relax,' David said.
'We are good together. I think we can sell this book for
serious money, nah?'
'Look, David, I really like you, but not like this, ok? I am
married. Come on, let's move on.'
He withdrew his hand and placed it on the steering wheel.
Ursula couldn't see his expression but she could sense his
frustration, as he had started to tap his fingers on the wheel.
'I don't want much. Come on, give me a little. I knew from
the first day you wanted it.'
'Did you now. Well, maybe you were wrong, David. Come
on, let's move on, or I will hail the next car coming, I
swear!'
'Hey, don't panic. I am not a rapist, by the way. No harm in
a fellow trying, is there? Come on, Ursula, nobody will

ever know that you gave your agent a kiss, hey. Nah, come on.'

'I will count to three. Drive on. I promise I will never say anything, but if you don't I am out of here and flagging cars down!'

'Alright, alright, don't get hysterical.'

David steadied himself, and they drove on. He didn't speak the rest of the way, and when he pulled into the long term at the rear of Kent station Ursula was delighted to see the security guard on patrol.

She only heard from David once after that. It was a short e-mail to say that he was no longer representing her on "The Sad Lady of Lislee." He also added that Hardy, on consideration, had withdrawn his offer as they judged the work to be "not publishable in its current form."

It wasn't a blow, as the thoughts of finishing the book became daunting. She wanted to do a happy ending where the rector conceded and allowed Anne to marry Robert Barry, but somehow she could not bring herself to believe in that storyline.

'How was Dublin anyway? Did you meet yer man Hardy?' Jack towered over her as she sat at the desktop.

'He wasn't very nice, Jack.'

'A lot of those fellas would skin you alive.'

'I know. That is true.'

'She is asleep, and I am going to watch the news. Are you alright up here? Is it too cold?'

'No, I am fine, Jack. You go on, I am happy here. Well done for getting her down.'

'She was lookin' at the painting that Evelyn gave you. She likes that one, doesn't she. Maybe the gull reminds her of herself, hey?'

'Maybe.' Ursula smiled.

When the light shines in through the turret, she feels the heat of the sun. It is secondary, so it heats her skin just right. Sometimes she stands in the same spot for hours just to receive the glow, and each morning she looks to see the sun come up over the hills and it spawns all life in the valley below, and she knows when darkness comes the creatures all hide and sleep.

The people who are close to her bring her food and give her shelter. They speak in easy words about dogs and cats and eat and sleep. Lately they had taken to showing her pictures, yes, to stop her bein' afraid of wild cows and tame horses.

Then they gave her the picture of the gull. Oh, stormy seas that flood the valley, sending raindrops in advance. And one single gull, alone, wind swayer, time stayer. The gull that defies the ordinary. Yes, these are the things that came to her on dark nights when she lay huddled and frozen in the corner. Her prison, the room in the tower of the temple of Lislee. Did she know that she was the sad lady? Did the animals know? And then what greater depth did her captors have, as they too only enjoyed their freedom temporarily? Life is only temporary. Is it this knowledge about time and its uselessness that made her escape, as she was unafraid of the consequences, as when nothing matters there are no consequences?

So when the straggler saw her standing at Coolim Cliffs, he thought it was someone normal. Little did he think that she would jump, and little did he know that she would fly like the single gull within the raging storm.

UNDER A BROKEN TREE

March 2002

Laura was my aunt through marriage, and she didn't marry my Uncle Trevor until he was sixty years old. She wasn't far behind him at fifty-seven. They were only married for five years when he died of throat cancer, and I might never have gotten to know her at all save for after my tenth birthday my mother used to bring me to visit her for a week every summer.

In fairness to Aunt Laura, she was a gem putting us up. Not that I was any trouble, mind, but my mother was in a different league. She was caustic and bitter, and ever since my father left her she was prone to bouts of irrational rage against men. Aunt Laura was well able for her though, and in times of crisis she would cry out, "Whist now, Maura, or you will disturb the peace."

She always said that and my mother, not sure of how to respond, usually shut up.

She lived in a modest house below Lislee Temple right where the valley started to rise so you could say it was elevated, yet it was no strain to walk up to the front door. From the upstairs window I could see all across the valley. I had a bird's eye view of the farms with the cattle and the winding hedgerows that bound them. Looking the other way I could see out beyond Coolbawn to Courtmacsherry Bay, and even as a child I had found it all wonderful, and I wanted to go out and play so I could smell the fresh air for myself and listen to the birds sing in the trees nearby. It was no doubt that Laura had a fondness for me, as I took myself out and made friends with the kids who lived in the area. If I wasn't out fishing I was herding cattle up Cuckoo Hill with Neil Sullivan, who became my best pal.

But I think Laura liked me most for dealing with life when subjected to my mother's delusions and her other afflictions. Though Mother gave out endlessly about Laura and accused her of stealing her brother's house she could never really get anything on her, as Laura lived in a permanent state of grace. Not that she was holy in any way but more that she had positioned herself as being above the prejudice of normality. She was ultra-practical and solemnly in control and it was almost like she had erected an electric fence around her person and nobody—not even my crazy mother—could break through.

When I grew up and went to Dublin to work the visits ceased, and eventually my mother succumbed to Alzheimer's before she died. Save for the odd card at Christmas, all contact with Aunt Laura ended. So I was surprised to receive the letter from Hayes & Harris, solicitors in Clonakilty. It was to sadly inform me that Aunt Laura had passed on, aged ninety-six years. I was even more surprised to find that she had left all of her worldly goods to me. So my drive south was filled with reflection, as I enjoyed the opportunity to revisit West Cork and see the world I had fallen so much in love with as a young boy.

I arrived at the house, and John Harris of Hayes & Harris was waiting for me. Now, I was expecting a mature austere man who was about to impart all the sad details of my late aunt's demise, but instead this thirty-year-old smart kid emerged from a BMW with his hand outstretched.
'Kevin O' Driscoll! John Harris. How are you–good!' he answered for me.
'Long journey down,' he said, walking up the pathway to the front door.

The house looked well. The windows sparkled in the
sunshine, and the flower beds were neatly groomed
enjoying the arrival of spring.
'A neighbour has looked after the place the last six months.
It is perfect if you want to stay here.'
He spoke like a country fellow who had been sent to a posh
school, his accent unrecognisable, but it was subliminally
smart and business-like.
'The neighbour has the place spotless, as you can see.
Evidently they were great friends. Anyhow, I have an
urgent meeting in Bandon so we can go through some stuff
now. You will just have to call by the office to sign all the
papers.'
Sitting at the kitchen table in the scullery, he unleashed a
zipped file that he had hidden under his arm. He ruffled
through some papers. I was trying not to be emotional and
it wasn't that I was sad, but memories of Aunt Laura and
my mother drinking tea at that same table came flooding
back.
'Ok, Mr O' Driscoll, here's the deal. She left you the house
and all its contents. She also left you twenty thousand euros
in savings she had made. Did you know that she was a nun
for over thirty years.'
'No,' I said.
'I had no idea. My mother never said anything.'
'She probably didn't know.'
 John Harris laughed.
'Nuns are sort of secret, aren't they?'
I didn't know that they were, but I just thought his
comments were disrespectful.
'Anyhow that's more or less it. She did leave some money
to cancer research too, but we can read through the entire
will when you drop by. Oh, and if you are going to stay
here you had better get some grub. The fridge is empty.'

He was on his feet packing up his papers and zipping up his bag.

'Friday at 2pm suit you?'

I wasn't sure what way to take him as he was very charming but he had this way of talking that made me feel his junior, even though I was most likely ten years his senior. He held out his hand for me to shake, which I did, but I made it short. Unbothered he said, 'Nice house. Probably worth a hundred grand. Small bit of land on the back. Not bad. You did well.'

I wanted to tell him that I didn't feel I did well, because it didn't matter to me. Not that I didn't need the money, mind. Things had been very tight since I got married. No, I just didn't look at it that way. He left revving his engine before departing down the narrow road like it was a racetrack.

However, I did take his advice and headed off to get supplies. I found all I needed in the Barryroe Co-op, which was only a mile or so from the house. It had the look of a place that had just sprung up in the middle of nowhere. I was paying for my goods at the till when an elderly woman with thick spectacles eyed me peculiarly. Every time I made eye contact she fixed on me with a lethal stare, so much so that I felt a little uncomfortable. When I had paid for my groceries she approached me. I noticed that her face was rutted with deep lines around her chin and up the sides of her nose.

'Are you in Laura's?' she said caustically, like she felt I was guilty of something.

'I am. I am her nephew, Kevin.'

The old woman's demeanor changed in an instant; she was no longer stiff and sour.

'Oh, Kevin, you gave me a fright! The last time I laid eyes on you, sure, you were only this high!'

I smiled at her warmly, and she beamed back at me. Then she started to play games.

'You don't know me, do you?'

I was about to say that I didn't and I really didn't want to waste time guessing, but she said, 'I am Nora Sullivan, Neil's mother, and you won't believe me, but he is running a big factory over in Chicago. They make tractors and all sorts, but he hasn't been home this long time. Four grandchildren he gave us. Of course you know about poor Peader; he has passed on. Gone three years next month.'

'Sorry to hear that. Great to hear Neil is doing so well, though. That must be a comfort for you.'

'Ah, it tis, but she isn't the best, ya know. She's a darky, and they are all a bit funny, aren't they?'

I was about to say no, they are not funny, like what the hell are you on about, but it really wasn't worth it.

'She went peacefully in the end. I used go see her every Sunday into Clonakilty. There she was sitting up in the bed, waiting to see what I brought her. My neighbours boys cut the grass for her, good lads they are, and I kept the house clean, but I have to say that for a long time when I went visitin' she didn't say much to me at all. She just sat there lookin' out the window like she was lost in her own world.'

'Old age, Mrs Sullivan. There are none of us getting younger.'

'True, Kevin boy. Listen, she gave me somethin' to mind for her, and she told me to make sure I gave it to you personally so I will. I will be around at eight o' clock. I don't want to miss Coronation Street and all of the goings on.'

She called at about five past eight and arrived with a package bound inside a manila envelope. I guessed she wanted to stay and make small talk, but I was tired and I told her that I was expecting an important call from Dublin.

She mumbled something under her breath, but then as she was leaving she turned back, dramatically saying, 'Whatever it is, it is very precious, boy, so mind it for God's sake.'

I put the package on the kitchen table and then actually took a call from my good wife. She was in poor form having been to the dentist that afternoon, so she didn't stay on very long. I was hungry so I made myself some scrambled eggs and toast on the gas hob—evidently they hadn't got around to disconnecting it yet—and I thought maybe it would be wise to keep it connected, as the idea of keeping the house as a summer home really appealed to me, especially when the kids came along. If they came along. But that was another matter altogether. After my food I helped myself to a well-deserved glass of wine, then I lit the fire using turf and some sticks. Mrs Sullivan had left them and there was also an ample supply of logs, but there was no coal. Soon the smoke bellowed up the chimney, and the flame and heat brought life to the place. After a few glasses of wine I went to the kitchen to fetch the package. I opened it to find a hardback notepad, and when I opened the notepad, I was surprised to see in her handwriting, "To Kevin, so as you will know me!" I turned the page and I read.

September 1922

It is hard for me to remember—so hard—but the day that Michael Dillon came down the mountain is one that I will never forget. I can assure you of that, as it was the day after my sixteenth birthday. He was weak but so handsome and maybe that is why Eileen let him in, for in truth she had no other reason to do what she did. Perhaps it was just her natural caring attitude; it was her way to care, and in a way

110

it was this that led us to live at the foot of the mountains. The Nephins are big black mountains, and we had a cottage with a few acres in the valley below. Down from the big black mountains he came. It was September in 1922, and the summer had left us with a terrible chill in our bones as the country was savaged by a dirty civil war. I was out in the back field walking Dawn. She hadn't been herself and she was off her food, and I dunno why but I looked up and there he was limping his way down the meadow. He had a rifle strapped over his shoulder, but he could hardly take the weight of it. When he got up close I could see he had dried blood caked to his face, and his cap and gabardine coat were wet and filthy. When he spoke his voice was quiet like, and I had to strain to hear him.

'Dat's a fine horse.'

Those words will live with me forever.

'She is,' I said.

'What happened to ya?'

He sat in the meadow grass. His leg could no longer sustain him, and he laid the rifle out 'til it was hidden. Dawn was taking to him, and she stuck her big head over his shoulder. He petted her gently on the mane, but then she took fright and moved away.

'I'm in de war. Tell me, girl, is der soldiers here?'

'Nah. Yer foot looks bad. Did you break a bone?'

'I twisted it. I wus runnin from soldiers up de mountain.'

'Is there soldiers up there?'

'Der is, an der is more of 'em comin'. But ya see dey shot me bruther, Danny. Dey killed 'im.' He allowed his whole body to fall into the meadow grass 'til I could just see the tip of his nose, and I knew by the way his head shook that he was crying. Just then Eileen arrived. She had been watching from the barn.

'Move away, Laura,' she commanded, and when I did she said, 'What's yer business here? There is nuthin' for ya here!' Sitting upright once more, he wiped the tears from the side of his face with his sleeve.

'Me name is Michael Dillon. I'm captain in de IRA, but I've busted me foot so I canee walk no more.'

So that was it. Eileen, for all her bravado, hadn't the heart to turn him away, and a few minutes later he sat by the fire drinking broth, and she immersed his foot in a bucket of cold water that I got from the well.

'It's a strange thing to be askin' a boy to fight a man's war, isn't it?' Eileen was pretending to be angry, but I knew that she was really just concerned.

'Up in those freezing cold mountains fightin', for what? What will be gained?'

'Dey wan us to accept de treaty, ma'am. We canee accept de treaty. Den we'll lose everythin'.'

'The treaty means nuthin' to the likes of us here. We will still be servin' Dr Dempsey and his horses no matter what. Look at you the state of ya, and you still a child!'

Michael looked at me like he needed to make sense of Eileen and her ranting.

'It's tem dat wanna break up de country an' its people wit it. De commandant says dey 'ill keep de people as slaves.'

'Slaves, is it?' Eileen said, emptying more water into the bucket. He grimaced.

'Cause de rich people ar behind de staters—wit de British. Maybe de church an' God knows who else. Dat's wat ur commandant says.'

'Was it ever any other way?' Eileen said caustically.

'Yer too young to be worried by politics. Who got in ta yer head, I would like to know.'

Michael watched her stir the broth and it was like watching a little boy admire his mammy, and for a moment I was so glad that he had come down from the mountain as suddenly the boredom that dominated our lives had lifted.

112

His foot was hardly improving over the next few days, and Eileen allowed him sleep in the armchair by the fire. That way he could rest his foot up on the hard chair. It was a sight to see him asleep, with a blanket up to his neck and his rifle standing against the wall behind him. It was comical, as it wasn't a soldier that he made at all; he just looked like a boy, all young and innocent. Eileen had threatened to put him out in the barn with the horses. She said things, like it wasn't really decent for him to stay indoors as we had to wash ourselves in front of him each morning, but in fairness to Michael he snoozed away or at least he pretended to be asleep. After a few more days of bathing in cold water his foot did improve, the swelling went down, and the redness went out of it. He looked better too. The blood had returned to his face, and the regular food seemed to bloat him 'til I could see that he was naturally a robust fellow and not the skinny boy that came down from the mountain. At night Eileen used to question him. At first I thought that she was being hard on him, but she wasn't really. I think she was trying to persuade him to up and go home, to go find his people and get out of the war. Michael was nothing if not a stalwart to the cause and his beloved commandant.

'Fellas younger dan me fought at de Somme,' he said, and Eileen, not flinching, retorted, 'Sure, isn't that the colonial thing to do, to fight wars and win medals? It is in their history, but it is hardly in ours.'

'Yer rite der, ma'am, but wer in grave danger an' if ya saw de viciousness of 'em ya wuld say 'm rite.'

Michael looked hard at her, and I could see his eyes steely clear underneath the lamplight. 'Dis Captain Stack killed me bruther. Poor Danny had no chance see, he wantin' him ta give names of fellas, tell 'em wher we wer hidin' out. But Danny said nuthin'. De captain took no pity either; he shot 'im dead in cold blood, back of de head.' Michael's voice started to shake, and Eileen, pretending she didn't notice, got up to the range to make tea. But then Michael said, 'Have nuthin' else, ma'am. Ders only me now an' de republic.' Eileen's voice softened and she simply said, 'I hope yer republic is worth it.'

Within a week Michael started to help around the yard, but he really helped himself when early one morning there was a right racket over at the henhouse and the fox that had bothered Eileen for weeks had broken through the fence again. She went charging with the doctor's shotgun, firing wildly and missing the animal and then hurting her shoulder in the process. Michael stood behind her, and ushering her out of the way he took aim at the escaping fox. He fired, and the fox was dead. Eileen looked at him in wonder.

'Wer nah like de staters. Wer well trained, ma'am.'

That night I had my bath in the kitchen and Eileen showered me with jugs of warm water. It drained down my back, and my skin was massaged by the heat of it. Eileen was going to throw Michael out but it was a bitter night, and she decided to leave him be after his heroics and it wasn't an option to send him up to our room where all our privates were. She put the tub behind him away from the fire so as he would have to strain himself to see me, but he didn't peek, not even once. He was quiet if anything, staring into the log fire like he was listening to the sizzle and the crackling of the wood. When she finished Eileen wrapped me in a towel, and he finally looked around.

'Make sure to dry under yer arms,' she said.

'Let it go, so,' I said.

'We will not with a man here.'

Eileen turned to see if Michael was looking and I let the towel go, and he looked at me in wonder his eyes moving up and down, and then Eileen bashfully turned back.
'Wrap up will you, yer not decent!'
And Michael looked away.
'Will you go and see if Dawn is calm? The wind and the rain disturb her.'
Michael was surprised as it was more my job, but he got up and still limping he went out in to the night.
'That isn't decent,' I said, 'but you let...' 'Ssh. Quiet! Never say dat, never!'
Eileen gripped my arms so tight that I pulled against her to be released.
'It is the price we pay. Remember, I told ya, I have to do it.' On seeing that she was hurting me, she eased her grip and I felt a tear slip down my cheek, and I was annoyed by it as I wasn't given to crying.
'De horse is grand. I put some crates up against de fence, I'll fix all properly in de mornin'. A fox will stay put dis night. It's ta stormy even for a fox.' Michael sat down by the fire again, and Eileen made me go up to the room to get dressed. When I came back she gave us all tea, and we pulled the hard chair close to the grate so as I could dry off.
'Winter is calling. It is startin' to blow, and when it does it never stops in this godforsaken place,' Eileen said.
'Aye,' Michael answered.
'As soon as me leg heals, I'll be up der in de snow.'
Michael's face took on a manly look in the flicker, and yet somehow it made Eileen look girlish.
'Whatever brings ya back up there?' she said. There was an uneasy silence so then I said, 'We can bring Dawn for a gallop in the mornin', Michael. We can go down the strand. Ya can ride Betsy Blue; she is a favourite of mine.'
Eileen looked at me sternly, but Michael's face lit up, 'As long as I can get up on her with me leg.'

'Ya will, of course,' I said, and Eileen shook her head as if she was overcome with sadness.

'Yis won't be goin' nowhere in this weather. You had better pray for better, child.'

'Yee don't know the weather, Eileen,' I said tersely. 'Even you don't know it.'

Michael, sensing my anger brewing, went, 'We can see in de mornin'. Miracles happen.'

'As long as the horses are fit to go to Newport on Friday, that is all that ails me,' Eileen snapped. I could have kissed Michael there and then, as Eileen was for swaying, and that had never happened before.

The following morning we got the last of the autumn sun, and the fields lit up. Michael was a good horseman, and we raced all the way along the gallops up by the high cliffs. Dawn led the way down the narrow furrow to the strand and Michael let Betsy Blue loose and she responded, and I had to push Dawn to keep up with her. Michael allowed his mount to splash in the surf, and I followed suit although I wasn't so sure that Dawn would like the water. She was nervous at first, but after time she seemed to enjoy it.

'Where did you learn to ride?'

'Keep tellin' ya, we wer well trained an' ridin' horses tis part of it, I rode Danny's mare. She wus a hard excitable yoke, an' I tamed her. She wanted dat kind touch. Come on, I'll race ya.'

And he was off and I in pursuit but I didn't catch him and Dawn was supposed to be one of the doctor's fastest horses, and I swore to myself not to tell him as the doctor might sell her off if he knew that Betsy Blue was faster. We stopped up by the cliffs, and we dismounted and lay in the meadow grass. I was listening to the sea beating against the rocks below. Michael sat up. He was chewing on a piece of

116

straw, and he took off his cap to allow the sun warm his head.

'Why ar ya goin' to Newport?'

'To get supplies and see the doctor about his horses.'

'Keep hearin' bout him.'

'He owns this place. Eileen works for him. She tends to his injured horses; he lets us live here, so.'

'Strange, two fine wimman like yis, don't 'ave yer own place.'

'Our father owed the doctor. Don't say a word to Eileen, but my father owed the doctor on account of the racing. He lost heavily, and then he started drinkin' so we had nuthin'. Anyways, the doctor gave him a choice, said we could live here to work off the debt. It might be worse.'

'Ya wud tink de doctor wud leave yis out of it.'

'My father was too ill to work, so it was all dat could be done.'

Michael lay down in the grass once again. He was thinking. I knew by how quiet he was.

'We go to Hennessy's grocery and Eileen gets me lemonade, and then every so often they come here.'

'Who cumes here?' Michael said, sitting up again.

'The doctor and Mr Hennessy. The doctor comes to check on his horses, and Hennessy, he brings hand-me-downs from his daughter and some homemade bread that his wife makes. They don't stay long but lately they have taken to drinkin' whiskey, you know, and to tell yah the truth it wasn't really right. They were tryin' to kiss and mess with Eileen, then they wanted to see us both, you know?'

'How wus it?' Michael said standing up, and Betsy Blue moved away with the fright.

'They asked us to undress a bit, like, and they looked at us but that was it. The doctor said that they needed to go, it was too late, but they were both drunk.'

Michael was quiet and he looked out over the cliffs, all the way across to Blacksod.
'Only a bastard wud do it, takin' advantage like dat!'
We mounted up, but this time we just cantered along as Michael didn't seem to be in any mood for fun.

*

The fire had died, and the room was suddenly cold. I thought of bringing the notebook to bed with me, but my eyes were burning after the journey and the reading just tired me more. I went up to the guest bedroom. It was at the front of the house, and I sat for awhile looking over the dark valley. It suddenly dawned on me that I had drunk the whole bottle of wine; perhaps this was an excuse for the sudden warmth I was feeling. The moon appeared from beyond a cloud, and the land lit up just for a few moments. I could see the outline of the temple and the old graveyard wall. The shadows soon became fields, and the trees removed themselves ghostly into the dark. I thought of her living here alone in this house, all those years alone, and now she had brought me back to her youth and to learn that terrible things happened to her. The civil war wasn't something that I had considered, as it wasn't taught in school. We knew it happened, but we never got to the detail. What dreadful events took place to have a young man—well, a boy really—up a mountain fighting against his own kind and spouting ideological guff that a fellow might only have heard in one of those Latin American countries? Surely the lad was prone to exaggeration; his brother was hardly summarily executed by the national army. I lay on the bed exhausted from my travels and my reading. Indeed, such was my fatigue that I fell asleep where I was and didn't wake up till early morning. The sun was shining through the window, and the sound of a cockerel someplace made me realise that it was morning

118

and I had omitted to undress, as I lay flat out on the bed fully clothed. So what was a man to do on a Thursday morning? Well, I got up to find there was lots of hot water as the fire had heated the tank, so I shaved and ran the bath. When I was clean and fresh I had breakfast of cornflakes and sausages and rashers all with sliced white bread, and I washed it down with steaming hot tea. I wanted to go for a walk up Cuckoo Hill but I allowed my breakfast digest first, and I picked up the notebook and continued to read.

*

In the end Eileen used two older horses to pull the cart. She insisted on holding the reins with me sitting beside her and Michael sitting lazily on the back. It was only after much deliberation that she decided to bring him at all, but somehow she worked it out that if she could pass him off as a visiting cousin he could stay longer and that people wouldn't be suspicious. I remember it was biting cold, and the news was that the national army had retaken Newport. There were countless warnings to watch out for landmines on the roads, and the talk was that the main road to Mulranny was treacherous. The side road was bumpy so we got little chance to pick up any speed, and we made our way to Newport slowly. It was better on the main road, but as we approached the town the soldiers had blocked the way.

'Let me talk,' Eileen whispered, and I could see Michael sit up nervously.

'What's yer business, ma'am?'

'On me way to see Dr Dempsey. I'm lookin' after his horses.'

'Dr Dempsey, is it? Who is this?' he said, pointing at me.

''Tis my sister, Laura.'

'Sister Laura, is it?' He then rounded the back of the cart to have a better look at Michael who pulled down his cap, casting a shadow over his face.

'Who is this, ma'am?'

Eileen turned towards the soldier.

''Tis me cousin, Michael. He's stayin' with us.'

'Staying with you, is it?'

'We 'ave ta meet de doctor. He is waitin' for us.'

'Dr Dempsey. Well, he is one of us, on ya go, so.'

Eileen screeched and the horses took off. Michael was staring back at the soldiers as they mingled.

'Don't stare,' Eileen warned.

'I think dey suspected somethin'.'

But we made it to Newport without further incident, and Eileen pulled the cart up by Hennessy's grocery. Mrs Hennessy was behind the counter. She was a big stout woman with massive breasts that sagged to her stomach. When Eileen approached she took a serious pose and leaned over the counter. I could see that she had a full moustache and the makings of a beard under her chin.

'Not over der, child,' she bellowed, looking over my shoulder. There was her daughter, Mary Kate. She was trying to place a display of vegetables.

'Keep 'em out of the light, girl!' her mother shouted. Then she finally reckoned Eileen, and she gave me a cursory nod, and then she looked on at Michael who was lost in the background.

'Hello Mrs Hennessy how are you all keeping?' Eileen asked.

''Tis fine, but since dey landed troops in Westport dey are restoring order, and the west will be free in no time. Good day, girl,' she said to me, and Mary Kate then knocked over one of the vegetable trays and the onions fell over the floor, much to her mother's displeasure. The girl was the cut of her mother in every way save for the facial hair, and she

looked around her awkwardly before chasing onions here
and there. Michael handed her one that had banged against
his boot. She took it from him shyly.

'Tis our cousin, Michael. He is down awhile, great with
horses. We are glad of him.' Eileen said to Mary Kate she
spoke loudly so Mrs Hennessy could hear! Mrs Hennessy
gave Michael the once over.

'I will see if himself is around, so. No point in delaying ya.
It's a wonder ya haven't been troubled by the irregulars.
Dey are starvin', good enough for dem!'

And off she went into the back to get her husband. When
she came back he was right behind her, his bald head
towering over her. It was a sight to see such a large woman
fade into the background. Eileen introduced Michael all
over again, and I wondered was she wise as Mrs Hennessy
kept eyeing him peculiarly. Eileen gave Mr Hennessy the
shopping list, and at once he took off opening jars and then
climbing a ladder to open tins.

'The doctor is in town!' he shouted from the top of the
ladder. 'He was with Father Kelly; serious business about
excommunicating irregulars. Fuckin' heathens anyways.
He told me to tell ya to hold tight, and we will come visit
next weekend. He wants to bring ya a two-year-old mare.'
Eileen waited for him to come back down the ladder.

'Does he not want to see me, so?'

'Nah, he will be with the priest all day. The priest wants to
denounce the irregulars from the pulpit. I think he needs the
doctor's guidance.'

'Give me two lemonades,' Eileen said, not hiding her
disappointment.

'He told me to charge him for dis; he will square up with ya
when he visits.'

Eileen looked at me, relieved, and Mr Hennessy gave me
my lemonade. Eileen offered the other one to Michael, but
he refused politely.

'Where is the lad from?' Mr Hennessy asked Eileen, but he was staring at Michael.

'We cum from de same parish,' Michael said without thinking, and Mr Hennessy as quick as you like said, 'And where would dat be?' Eileen, going red, said, 'You know well where we hail from. Sure, aren't ya from the same county yerself?' The conversation was interrupted by noise from outside, and Mr Hennessy lifted the hatch and pushed by Mary Kate to see what all of the commotion was about. He stood at the doorway, and then he shouted at some passer-by and we could hear, 'The captain is back with two dead bodies.'

'Two irregulars down, so yer man says. That's Hickey, the cabinet maker's son. He would know alright.' Mr Hennessy said. I looked at Michael; he had gone rigid, and for a moment I was fearful that he might lose all his sense and go charging out the door, so I said, 'It is a terrible thing, Mr Hennessy, to be takin' the lives of men and for folk to be gloatin' over it.'

'They will get little sympathy in dis house, girl,' he said, walking back beyond his counter. He looked at me like he was surprised that I could speak at all.

'Someone's son, Mr Hennessy,' Eileen said, and he gave her a loathsome look.

'We had three staters dragged up the street on a cart last Tuesday, not twenty years old any of 'em. Shot dead. It is the end of law and order. Someone has to pay. This Captain Stack is the man to sort it.' Michael went to say something but Eileen, pushing her way by him, said, 'We must go, we need to be back before dark.'

'God's speed. So we will bring ya the two-year-old,' Mr Hennessey said.

Outside the street was busy and a small crowd had gathered, most of them leaning on the wall by the river.

The troops were marching towards us, the leading officers on horseback. In the middle of them a horse drew a single cart. As they approached Michael stiffened; then he whispered to me, 'Dats 'im. Dats Stack.' The captain came by us. He was tall with a crop of grey hair under his cap, but he was portly for a soldier and he looked around eyeing the faces in the crowd triumphantly. His entourage was led by a younger thinner officer who was also on horseback. He was followed by about twenty soldiers with one pulling the horse and cart. The soldiers looked miserable, stopping abruptly at the officer's command.

'See here!' the captain shouted, and then some of the local children tried to get near and see the bodies, but I could see them as plain as day and I will never forget their fish dead eyes as they lay helpless. They were lying over each other, their clothes removed. They were left only in their underwear.

'Since we landed in Westport we are winning bit by bit. It is only a matter of time before we hunt these scoundrels down. Sergeant Dunne here knows the task we set ourselves, but look at him. He doesn't flinch. We will be back up in those mountains again very soon, so any of you here—any of you who sympathise with these irregulars who, by the way, have no mandate—tell your friends we are coming after them. They may give up now if they want their lives spared. Remember, next week it will be too late.' The captain's horse was spooked by the noise of a motor car coming from Westport, and he kicked it hard to steady it. I noticed the sergeant grimace at his action. The entourage moved on slowly, the troops passed by, and Eileen kept our horses steady until the noise died down.

Michael was quiet all of the way home and even later when we reached the cottage and he carried in the supplies, but when he sat by the fire I noticed that he eyed his rifle.

123

'I'll be headin' back up de mountain soon. Me leg is improvin'.'

Eileen was making tea, but she stopped what she was doing and she didn't chastise him as I thought she might. No, she just walked over to him, and she rested her hand on the side of his cheek.

'Wait a bit till it heals fully' was all she said.

*

My walk up Cuckoo Hill was wasted in the sense that even the sounds of the birds and the rattle of the wind couldn't distract my brain from searching over the words I had read. The hill got steeper, and in my mind's eye I had a vision of the dark Mayo Mountains and what it must have been like approaching winter and with a full scale civil war going on. When I reached the top of the hill the world opened up, and in the distance the ocean, and in between hundreds of acres of lush farmland, and it all seemed so calm. I turned left and walked along the meandering road. I was still wondering where my Aunt Laura's story might lead me as I crossed the fields to Coolim Cliffs, and I felt the wind chill against my face. I no longer saw her as my greying old aunt; now I saw her as a young feisty girl of sixteen, headstrong, seeking out a meagre living on a small isolated farm in the west of Ireland. I wondered, was it the same wind that blew down the cold mountains to touch her face? I think it was then that I made the decision to hold on to the house, as reading her story taught me that she was too important and there was no way I could allow her to go out of my life. On my walk back I stopped to look over the Atlantic out beyond Dunworley. The landscape was suddenly dark, and only the hidden light beyond the clouds brought it authenticity, as the rain formed black lines like I used to see in old cine reels. Going back down Cuckoo Hill it started to rain and the gullies filled with water, and when

I reached the bottom the water became a torrent crossing the narrow road like a fast river. When home I lit the fire and made myself a coffee before sitting comfortably to read once again.

*

The doctor had a big black car; I could see it from a mile away. It came over the ridge and down the narrow track. Behind him the lorry with the horses blew smoke that curled into the air in puffs that dissolved against the grey sky. The lorry was noisy coming into the yard, and Eileen went out to meet them. She was eager to talk to the doctor about his horses and also to discuss money. I saw Michael. He was over by the barn; he had been hammering nails into a piece of wood that he had used to reinforce the water trough. I could tell, even though I wasn't close by him, that he wasn't happy with visitors. To him they were suspicious and dangerous.

'Not a bad day,' Hennessy said.

He carried his hat in his hand, and his bald head led the way from the car. He went to the rear to take out a hamper of groceries, and then he carried them straight into the kitchen. The doctor was slow getting out of the car on account of his bad leg. He had suffered the injury when a horse fell on him while he was out jumping.

'Mattie, we will let them out,' he said, ignoring all and addressing the man driving the lorry. The small man went about his business quietly but with diligence as the lanky doctor looked on. As always he was dressed for the occasion with wellington boots and sports trousers tucked neatly into them. His jacket was strong wearing, and his tweed cap all lent to the appearance of a country gentleman. There were three horses, and the two-year-old looked frightened and underweight.

'She is eating nothing,' the doctor said as Eileen slipped a tie around her, and the horse settled straight away. I went to tend to the other horses when Hennessy, lifting another box from the car, said, 'Mary Kate sent on a few things.' Hennessy wasn't dressed for the country at all. His ill-fitting suit looked out of place, and his shoes were already destroyed by the muck in the yard. He brought the box of hand-me-downs into the kitchen, and I couldn't help but think that if any of Mary Kate's clothes fitted me then I was in a right stew. The doctor went off to the barn with Eileen to tend to the horses, and when Michael saw them coming he moved on to finish some work on the boundary fence. The afternoon was closing in and then Mattie left with the lorry, its noise scaring the animals and drilling in my ears as it left through the wide gate.

'Mary Kate says they should all fit yah, since ya are growing at such a rate. It is prettier yer getting too.' Hennessy had started on the whiskey. At first he poured just a small sup into the cup as we had no glasses, but then he poured way more the second time, and then I noticed he had another full bottle tucked under the clothes.

'Ya must be eighteen now, hey?' he said, lookin' me up and down.

'Mary Kate is twenty next week. It is catchin' up on her ya are, and you have a beautiful woman's body.'

He was spitting around his mouth, and it was then I realised that this wasn't his first drink of the day and most likely the doctor had joined him. So then I started to worry about Eileen in the barn.

'I'd better go see Eileen about the horses,' I said casually but he was drinking more whiskey, pouring it liberally now.

'Have a drop,' he spluttered, 'it will duy ya no harm.'

When I went to leave, he blocked my passage to the door. 'Where would ya be goin'? Sure, we are havin' a bit a fun.'

'I have to go to Eileen to tend the horses.'

'She is well able with the horses. Don't ya worry, Doc Dempsey is mindin' her!'

He put his big hairy hand against my breast and started to push, and then he grabbed me and pulled me tight against him. The next thing was I felt him lift me onto the corner of the table, and his hands were pulling at my pants. All the time I could feel him press against me and he was hard on, and I smelled his stinking breath as he bit into my neck. Suddenly the kitchen door flew open, and it was Eileen followed by the doctor. Eileen was red in the face, the likes of what you only see after an argument.

'You are starting without me,' the doctor said to Hennessy who backed off and released me so as I could straighten myself.

'What are you playin' at?' Eileen shouted, rushing to protect me. Hennessy, laughing, took another cup from the dresser and poured the doctor a whiskey.

'Now, now, Eileen,' the doctor said, 'we were discussing things on the way over here, in between dodging landmines and such. Laura must be old enough to do what you do for us. You know I let you live here. This is my place. You hardly think you earn enough to live here by just tending to my horses, do you now, Eileen? We need a little more for this arrangement to work.'

'You can do what ya like to me, but ye will not touch her!' The doctor moved over to stand beside me.

'She is so pretty, Eileen, and sure she is a grown woman.'

'She is barely sixteen!'

'I think a girl in the town got married recently and she was only sixteen, isn't that right, Hennessy?'

'It is, and they get married younger up the country,' Hennessy said gleefully.

'Right, Eileen, it is your call. You choose to live here. You give us a little cooperation. If not we can send the bailiffs in, and you will be on the street with your father's debt choking you. It is your choice: a little fun this afternoon or the road. What is it, you say?'

Eileen sighed, her eyes swelling with tears.

'You can take whatever it is from me—God knows you have tried it before—but ya will not touch her. I will see the road first and take on all of my father's debts, and remember, Doctor, ya will have nobody to tend to those horses.'

The doctor remained calm. He drank the rest of his whiskey down and Hennessy refilled it immediately, and then the doctor walked over to where we stood and he studied Eileen's tearful face. Without warning he slapped her hard across the cheek, and Eileen kept her head tilted in the position that he had forced it into. Slowly she straightened up, and then he slapped her again. This time she straightened up defiantly.

'Maybe you just don't have a say!' he shouted angrily and the next thing I was lifted and pulled up the small stairs to the bedroom, and Eileen was dragged after me, and they pushed each of us on to Eileen's bed.

'You will not defy me, bitch!'

The doctor started to pull at Eileen clothes until he ripped at her blouse, and her left breast showed. Hennessy started to lift my frock as he did before. He grabbed at my underwear, this time pulling my pants down to my knees.

'Wat da yah think yer doin'?' Michael stood at the bedroom door, his rifle pointed at the doctor's heart. Eileen was on her feet. She stood by the small window partially blocking the last of the afternoon light. All was dim.

'We were having a joke,' the doctor said meekly.

'Yes,' Eileen said.

'There is no trouble. We were havin' a laugh!'

The doctor pulled back his coat, revealing a small pistol.

'I carry this save we meet some irregular thugs. I am not afraid to use it,' he warned.

'Sure, it was just a joke, Michael. Put the rifle away. Come on, we can all go down to the kitchen.' Eileen pleaded, but the doctor smiled at Eileen, turning his back temporarily on Michael. Eileen, watched the doctor, he took a step backwards, and then all hell broke loose. The doctor fired his pistol, but Michael caught him full on in the forehead and he collapsed to the ground. Hennessy threw his hands in the air and shouted,

'No, don't!'

But Michael shot him bang in the chest and his blood spurted and hit the side wall, and it was then I saw Eileen as she lay pale white on the floor. The bullet from the doctor's pistol had blown a hole through her throat. It was like a mist had descended, and for a few minutes all was in slow motion. All was unreal, and I just couldn't accept that my lovely Eileen had been taken from me.

The next few days got lost in a haze, and I have distant memories of helping Michael clean the blood off the walls. I remember sitting in the meadow at the rear of the cottage, watching him dig Eileen's grave. The earth was hard from the frost, and the spade hit and spun against the solid ground. The harder he pounded the worse it got, 'til I feared the head of the shovel would break off. Eventually Michael found a softer patch at the edge of the vegetable garden, and we buried her at that spot, and I was pleased because I knew that in the spring buttercups and daises grew there. I watched him dig tirelessly, and I longed for him to speak but he hadn't spoken a word since the shooting. At first we had left all as it was in the bedroom, and we just sat by the fire in complete silence 'til sleep came, and when I woke it was morning, and he cooked eggs, and he made toast with a fork at the fire.

Later we carried the bodies of the doctor and Mr Hennessy, and Michael placed their bodies in the doctor's car. I sat in the passenger seat and Michael drove the car across the fields to the cliffs, and then he let off the handbrake and we pushed hard 'til the car toppled over the cliff, and we heard it break against the rocks below. Then Michael lay on the flat of his belly to look over and he shocked me when he eventually said, 'It tis sinkin', Laura. Will give us some time; as sure as anythin' they will be cumin' to find 'em. We 'ave to pack up and go.'

'Go where?' I said. 'I can't go and leave poor Eileen. It wouldn't be right, Michael.'

'We gotta go, luve. De staters 'ill be all over here. We canee be here wen dey cum, or I'm a goner. Nah, we gotta go up de mountain, pack as much as we can carry, take de two best horses.'

'Yer right, Michael, but why did you show 'em the rifle? Jesus, it was bad, but at least Eileen was alive.'

He looked at me, his deep blue eyes hurting.

'I did de only decent ting a fella cud do. Yis wud have been slaves forever, bound to der will en notions. Who knows wat deyed've done to yis? Slaves forever, Laura. He wus tryin' to shoot me, so he wus. Den 'is pistol fired killin poor Eileen. We gotta hurry, Laura!'

I saddled Dawn and Betsy Blue, and Michael packed as much food and warm clothes as we could fit into the saddlebags. He topped up the water bottles with water from the well, and we headed off along the narrow track that ran from the meadow. I had left food and water for the other horses, knowing they wouldn't be alone for long. When we reached the first ridge I steadied Dawn to look back down the mountain, and the smoke drifting from the chimney made me sad, as it was a stark reminder of the life I had once lived. I must have been looking awhile as Michael

130

came back for me, and Betsy Blue rubbed nostrils with Dawn.

'She is buried there, Michael, and I have this awful feelin' that I will never see our little cottage again. I can't believe she is gone. She is gone forever, Michael!'

'Tis a shock, girl. Cum on, gotta get up de mountain before dark. Don't look back no more.' He took Dawn by the reins and we went on, and when I looked around again I could no longer see the cottage or the smoke coming from the chimney. As we climbed all I could see were the massive peaks and the dark valleys above, and when darkness fell it got bitterly cold. Michael found us shelter in a wood by a fast flowing stream. He made sure I had the heavy blanket, and in the middle of the night I wasn't sure if he had enough warmth so I threw my arm over him and hugged him tight. He just stayed motionless, and I fell back asleep to the sound of his soft breath.

The next day we climbed higher and the air was colder, and in the afternoon it began to snow. It was just a few flurries at first but then it fell heavily, and the horses moved slowly through it. We came to a high rocky outcrop, and suddenly two men appeared carrying rifles. I was struck by how young they were. They looked even younger than Michael.

'It is you, Michael Dillon. We thought ya were dead!'

'Nah, wus me poor bruther dey got.'

'Aye,' the young man said.

I strained my neck to see him, as he towered above me. They had a lovely fire in the camp, and the men were sitting round it tending to their weapons.

Each one acknowledged Michael, but none of them got up or made a fuss.

'You should be dead,' the commandant said, and Michael, dismounting, said, 'Dey got Danny.' The commandant walked over and shook his hand I noticed he was

131

dishevelled with the makings of a beard, he was small but stocky which gave him some gravitas.

'Who is she?'

'Dats Laura. She is wit me. Is a long story, sir.'

'Come get her warm. It is bitter. We have only a little food, and we are short of all else. The bastards are grinding us down. They have British guns and an endless supply. It is only a matter of time. You know they got Kilroy?'

'Nah, I didn't. See, I was hurted. Laura gave me refuge, sir.'

The commandant ordered a man to bring us steaming broth that was really good. The fire soon warmed my bones, and for the first time in many days I felt human again.

'We are losing this war, Michael,' the commandant said. 'What we are not losing in the field they are executing, and now the church wants to excommunicate us men who are just fighting for their country. Aye, and it's a wonder a fellow could have any religion left to see his country plundered by the wealthy classes. They will make slaves of us for sure. They will have only a part of the country, and the British will mind their interests in the North. All so the men of property, the shopkeepers and merchants, can make their profits!'

Michael bowed his head as he reflected on the commandant's words. It was getting dark and the fire fought valiantly against the tyrannical crosswind, and the men were throwing blankets over themselves.

'We wer just havin' a look round, Commandant. We wer headin' back to camp. Dey cum on us sudden, like, a few of 'em on horses. Den Danny en me ran for our lives. We ran over a ridge en on down by a small lake; we hid in de reeds. Den dis Captain Stack, he pulls up wit 'is big white horse. He screams at us ta cum out. Danny says to me "Stay still, like" so I do. En de next ting is Danny walks out all brazen like. En he laves me wit de rifle. 'Dis Captain

Stack gets his corporal to knock Danny around en shout at 'im. Danny never moves, even wen de corporal hit 'im wit de butt of 'is rifle. Danny said nuthin', 'is hed streamin' wit blood, so den dis Captain Stack gets off de horse en puts 'is pistol ta Danny's skull, en he wants names en de details of wher ya's are hidin'. But still Danny says nought, no word. All de time I 'ave de captain in me sights, can see 'im tru a gap in de reeds, but I canee do it, Commandant. I was scared but Danny made me swear not to do anythin', just to wait for him. To be honest I wus confused, sir.'

The commandant gave Michael a cup with whiskey and he offered me some too, but I refused and Michael just sipped at his.

'I hear the coward has taken refuge over by the black lake. He has the Dowling twins with him. His idea of comfort but they are half daft, and when the soldiers go on patrol it leaves him open with just two or three guards and they might be drunk. Yah may get yer revenge, Michael, but we are done. Tomorrow I will bring the men down to Newport. There is talk of an amnesty, so you may do it, or stay here and starve or be shot.'

I could see that Michael was overcome with sadness on hearing the defeatist words of his hero, Commandant Maxwell. Later on I heard him rouse in his sleep and cry out once or twice.

I awoke to find the men were packing. They looked tired and some of them shook hands like they were saying goodbye to each other, and Michael was pleading with the commandant.

'Ya can take her down, sir, it tis nah place for a girl,'
The commandant was considering his request when I said, 'I will be goin' nowhere. Not without you, Michael. And if it is to die I will die with you, but I will not be separated from you. I swear, I will break free just to follow you!'

So that was it. We took off and we crossed several valleys of deep snow and the horses were slow, and once I had to lead Dawn uphill for a distance and it tired me out whilst Michael waited at the top of the ridge overlooking the black lake. We looked down on the timber fisherman's lodge, now the headquarters of Captain Stack. Michael surveyed the scene for at least ten minutes before he said, 'I can take 'im. You see wat the commandant gave me.' Michael lifted the saddle cloth, and there pinned under the strap was a sawn-off shotgun.

'Ya see, Laura, it twill take 'im while I am still ridin'. Won't know wat's hit 'em.'

'You can't, Michael, there will be too many of 'em. Ya will be killed!'

I pleaded with him, but he didn't listen to me. He allowed me go with him to the edge of the wood. I could see the lodge clearly and there was a distant sound of music like a gramophone was playing. Then he hid me and Dawn. He told me to stay still and not to move, and if staters came by I was to just say that I was orphaned and lost. He kissed me gently on the cheek when he was leaving, and I tried to kiss him back on the lips but he avoided that. When he was gone I felt such a loneliness that I had to tie up Dawn and go see what was happening ,and I watched him from no more than twenty yards away. The fishing lodge was close to the lake shore, and Michael trotted Betsy Blue right up to where a single lamp burned in its window. He fired through the window, smashing the lamp and starting a small fire. Then he did a complete circle on Betsy Blue and there was a sound of commotion coming from inside the lodge. Michael fired again; this time a man fell wounded through the window, smashing the panes of glass. Michael did another circle on Betsy Blue and I heard gunfire and the snow around Michael was disturbed by bullets, but he just kept circling on the horse and bringing her out of range.

Eventually the door of the lodge kicked open, and the half-dressed Dowling twins emerged. They ran towards the lake screaming, and then the dishevelled Captain Stack appeared. He was, only wearing trousers and his vest but he ignored the biting cold. Michael brought Betsy Blue nearer. I could see he had the shotgun resting by his side.

'Can you explain this disturbance?' the captain shouted. 'I was having a little entertainment when you butted in, young man. Can you explain yourself?'

'I'm Michael Dillon, Captain. I'm comin' ta see ya abt me bruther, Danny. Ya shot 'im in de head. Ya remember dat, don't ya?'

'He was a traitor. We have orders to shoot traitors on sight.'

'Nah, he wus no traitor. He' wus a soldier in the Irish Republican Army, fightin' for freedom. Fightin' for de citizen!'

'You traitors are all Bolshies, hah! We will all be equal, will we?'

Just then a soldier came round the side of the lodge. He had his rifle cocked, and he took aim directly at Michael.

'Lest we're one wit de people!'

Michael shouted and fired simultaneously. The soldier fell dead into the snow. The captain flinched, but Michael could see he wasn't armed.

'You wouldn't shoot an unarmed man,' the captain said.

'Might if I wus as low as yah.'

'We have orders to kill all the traitors that don't surrender.'

The captain was at the edge of the wooden veranda, and Michael was no more than ten feet away from him. Betsy Blue took a sudden turn, and Michael, surprised, tried to steady her. The captain, seizing the moment, went for his pistol. He had concealed it in the back of his belt just above his backside. The shot was loud, and I can still remember it piercing through the air. Betsy Blue fell, sinking, into the snow. The white of the snow was soaked with red and I started to run towards them, and as I ran I saw the captain stand over Michael who was prostrate on the ground, the snow threatening to engulf him as it had started to fall heavily once more. The captain stood rigid, taking deliberate aim at Michael's head.

'Traitors!' the captain shouted.

Just as I got to them, I saw the captain's face explode and blood spurt through the air. It mingled with the falling snow, giving the world odd colours, and it is only when he turned his body did I see that Michael had blown half his face off. The glistening barrel stuck up from the snow like a piece of piping. I had no time to mourn for Betsy Blue. I was too busy going to retrieve Dawn so as we could make our escape. Escape we did, leaving the captain's body behind us and listening to the wailing of the Dowling sisters as we crossed the ridge. Dawn carried us as best she could, but then the snow got too deep. Michael dismounted and pulled her by the rein. We must have been some sight crossing those desperate valleys and ridges, just us and the snow and the mountains.

*

On Friday I signed all the papers in Hayes & Harris, and this time I was greeted by the older and more serene Mr Hayes. We went through the formalities quickly, and when I was leaving he shook my hand warmly.

'She was a very feisty woman, and she knew what she wanted,' he said. 'It was all very clear. I suppose if you are a nun for all of those years it rubs off, the old conservative nuns.'

I wanted to tell him how wrong he was but I saved it, as what was the point? He didn't know anything about my Aunt Laura or who she was and from where she came. I bought myself some more wine, and once I had the house suitably warm I sat to read the final pages of her memoir.

*

It stopped snowing as we made our descent through the last of the big valleys, but Michael stopped dead in his tracks as we climbed again. There among the rocks lay the bodies, at least ten if not more. He climbed the slippery bank feverishly, but even from where I was I could see their faces. The men we had said goodbye to at the campfire earlier that day the commandant amongst them, blood dried to his frozen face. Most of them had been shot at close range, it was obvious from their head wounds, but the bodies nearest the summit had been shot in the back, possibly as they made to escape. Michael came back to me tearful and weary.

'Tis all over now,' he said, and we went on with him leading Dawn. By now we were both exhausted, and the hunger was biting, and I found myself drifting in and out of sleep, but then inexplicably Michael stopped pulling at the horse and Dawn stopped, and I heard the sound of horses. A young officer who said his name was Dunne shouted, 'This man is unarmed. Arrest him, and take the girl.' The soldiers, all on horseback, made a circle around us. Corporal Dunne took Michael's sawn-off shotgun and, after studying it for a minute, dropped it into the deep snow 'it disappeared so fast. They brought us down the mountain, and then they separated us and that was it. I never laid eyes on Michael Dillon again. The soldiers fed me and then asked me questions, but I pretended to be in shock and unable to speak so eventually Sergeant Dunne released me to the nuns who had their convent down the street. I am not sure of what happened to Michael, as there is much hearsay and very little evidence. All I know is that he was brought to Westport and then transferred to Athlone by train.

Evidently there was a mix-up in registering his details, and the duty officer either mistakenly or deliberately entered the wrong date of birth, and Michael was listed as eighteen years old instead of the seventeen he actually was. Michael spent the Christmas of 1922 in jail, and he had been there just over a month when one dark frosty morning he was taken out along with two other boys and shot. He had no immediate family left, so it was only later that Republican sympathisers got his body and it was reinterred in the small graveyard on the road to Mulranny from Newport. People know it because it lies peacefully beside Grace O' Malley's castle. As for me when I retired from teaching I went to visit his grave, and I placed a single rose on it, and his headstone was simple. It just said:

'Captain Michael Dillon—IRA –Died January 1923'

And that was it. I taught in the convent in Cork for all of those years until I finally met a man with whom I could find peace with, and I did, although we both knew that I had only one great love. It gave me a great peace to find Michael's grave and place my flower on it. I suppose looking back I didn't have a great life, but I had an interesting one. The nuns were good about helping me give Eileen a proper burial, but I am afraid whilst the nuns were good to me that I wasn't a very good nun. I look at my time spent in the order as one of atonement rather than anything spiritual, as even to this day I hardly feel religious. By the way, there was never a mention of either the doctor or Mr Hennessy again. Their bodies were never recovered and in the times that were in it, I doubt if either of them were sadly missed.

*

It was time for me to head back to Dublin where my wife awaited me with her sore gums and brittle humour. I was in no rush, so I walked down to the old graveyard by Lislee Temple. It was a beautiful sunny day, and I walked among the lonely graves until I found Laura's. The inscription read.

'Trevor McCarthy died aged 65 years, his wife Laura aged 96 years' and then the simple lines of Yeats' poem:

Like the moon her kindness is,
If kindness I may call
What has no comprehension in't
But is the same for all
As though my sorrow were a scene
Upon a painted wall.

So like a bit of stone I lie
Under a broken tree.
I could recover if I shrieked
My heart's agony
To passing bird, but I am dumb
From human dignity.

William Butler Yeats

How little would anyone know just from reading that inscription. There was nothing about the woman who saw the shaping of a state through violence. A woman who witnessed first-hand the defeat of an ideology and the powerlessness of an earnest few against insurmountable odds.

'Ireland does not want a change of master. It would be folly to destroy English tyranny in order to erect a domestic tyranny that would need another revolution to free the people. The Irish Republic stands therefore for the ownership of Ireland by the people of Ireland. It means that the means and process of production must not be used for the profit or aggrandisement of any group or class.'

Liam Mellows whilst awaiting execution 1922

ON THIS ALMIGHTY ROAD

It is the wind that matters most, and it only matters because it blows all of the time. Every day it blows down the main street, taking everything with it. All of the birds and the branches of trees. It blows open unsecured doors and lifts plastic bags from the hedgerows, and it teases the bunting they put up for the festival. Yet somehow I am drawn to it, as it makes a flapping sound, deep and dark. It disturbs the peace, and for a moment it reminds me of imminent danger. During the festival, the people come out of the drains. They slither from the alleys, and fresh-faced women line the pavement cheering and laughing. Children run races and play tennis tournaments. It is summer, and the village celebrates. I love to stand in the middle of the street, the wind against my face. It burns me like a blow heater, and it sends me under the sheets. I wish those fresh-faced women were with me underneath the blankets where I hide from the wind, and the women follow me there and ask me questions from their treasure maps.
"Imagine finding you here."
They all say the same thing, but each woman has a different look. It is like some say it seriously, and others are laughing when they say it. After that it is business as usual. Get up out of bed. Shower, using two towels to dry myself, one for my head and one for my body. But when I am dressed where do I go? The cold bar across the street where unless you sit on top of the fire you will freeze and I know that I have to brave the wind to reach it. I check the funds. They are low. Surprise, surprise. Funds are low, time to go, but funds are low.

Then I brave it and go over, and I crawl under the wind and I meet Frank Holland, the owner, and Albert Byrne. I knew Frank and I didn't know Albert, and then Frank says,

'Hello, Harry,' and then my life changes forever. The bar is covered with dust, and the old beer mats are glued to the empty tables. The draught from the front door darts through our bodies, and Albert pulls up the collar of his coat to save his neck. He admits to many things, like that he reads the Examiner and that he is a "Blueshirt,' as was his father and three of his father's brothers. He tells me that Blueshirt is like Latin; it is a dead expression from a dead language. I argue that it is making a comeback. Frank is interested at first, but then he is distracted by the captain who sits tamely by the fire. He is warming his bones and complaining about his gout. Frank says 'He is bad enough with diabetes.' And Albert says, 'Fucking shinners…will be the death of me. Like, how do people give them a vote with all of the disappeared and that Gerry Adams?' And I go, 'The fuck with Gerry Adams, what about you Free State bastards and that Blueshirt, Enda Kenny?' Frank intervenes. 'My father was a Blueshirt and proud of it, boy!' And then I go, 'What has Gerry Adams got to do with the disappeared?' And Albert goes back to me. 'Didn't he order it?' And Frank says, 'He did.' And I say, 'Who says so?' And Albert, smug, says, 'Common knowledge.' I hesitate but then shout, 'Common knowledge, my bollix! If they had anything on Adams, sure, wouldn't he be arrested?' Albert, challenged by my point, picked up the Examiner for inspiration but there was none coming, so I decided to finish him off.

'You see, they have nothing on him! Not a thing! This is just a Free State hatchet job.'

The captain shouted over, 'He is up to his tits in it. He knows wher all the bodies are!' But when I look at the captain, he is staring at his left leg like he was wondering would it carry him whenever he decided to walk. Albert pretends to read the Examiner but I know he is fooling, as his eyes are moving much too quickly to actually read.

143

Frank starts to go on about the silage and how the ground is too wet yet, and Albert tells him that it is very quiet around and wonders why, to which Frank replies, 'I dunno, I suppose there is no money. Those that have it won't spend it; they are saving. And those that haven't got it are fucked, and the only fellas we get in here are poor, and, sure, they run out of cash after a few days, and they stay in too.' I said, 'The country's fucked, Frank, and it is a fact that people on welfare will spend all of their money locally, whereas the better off stay in and save, so if it is a better class of customer you are after you may as well forget it. Not going to happen anyway.'

Frank looked at Albert who was still pretending to read the Examiner.

'We are in recovery,' Albert said suddenly.

'It will take time but we are going the right way, and it is a pity that we weren't in power when the other yobbos had it. I might still have a business. Sure, the FFrs fucked us.'

'They fucked all of us!' Frank yelled from the fireplace where he bypassed the captain to stoke the coals.

'Fucking FFrs shud be ashamed of wat dey did,' the captain said quietly.

'You are as bad as each other.' I went, but as quick as a flash Albert turned his big white head to me and snarled.

'I had three supermarkets, boy, and they took them all off of me one by one. Them and the legals who are cunts as well!'

Frank shook his head, advising me to be careful.

Then Albert, lightening up, said, 'I will go a brandy, Frank, and a pint for my good communist friend. He is going to tell us all about North Korea. Is the weather good? I hear the brandy is great. Ha ha, hee hee!' Albert was pleased with his joke, but I was having none of it.

'You haven't a clue,' I said.

'You get all the news from RTE, and that rag you are
reading. No wonder your head is full of shit. Do you think
they are telling you the truth?' Frank put the drinks in front
of us. Albert turned to me in amazement; he went, 'Why,
do you think they are making it up?' I said, 'Yep, they put
their own slant on everything 'til all you hear is what they
want you to hear.' Frank rubbed his forehead, and then he
placed both his hands on the counter.
'It is as near the truth as ye will get. Don't tell me those
shinners are telling the truth. They are not, so you can make
your own mind up, but RTE is as good as it gets.' And then
Albert interrupted.
'Is it paranoid you are?' I was supping my pint now, and
Albert was examining his brandy like he was expecting to
find things floating in it.
'I am not paranoid. I just don't believe their slant on things.
They are pro government and banks and all the shit that has
us where we are. It isn't honest analysis. That is why the
country is fucked.'

I would like to think that I had the last word, but I didn't.
The conversation went on with Albert arguing like fuck and
the captain and Frank throwing in their two pennies' worth.
It was the first in what became a series of arguments and
discussions. The same words were always bandied about:
Ireland; recession; fucked, banks; North Korea;
communists; capitalism; neo-liberalism; pensions; and
social welfare, along with Fine Gael, Fine Fail, Labour, and
Sinn Féin. To be honest I found it frustrating in that I had
many ideas, but I was better off writing them down. When
it came to saying stuff, I more or less bottled it. Albert, for
all his misplaced adherence to mainstream politics, was far
more eloquent than me. He would lay the Examiner on the
counter and speak out and when he spoke people listened,
but when I spoke people turned off saying there he goes

again, and if they were bored they didn't bother to listen to me at all. Whatever about our misgivings for each other, and even allowing for the fact that we were polar opposites, I became close to Albert as beneath his abrasive crusty nature there was something of an enigma. He had once been super wealthy and the king of his castle; now he was ruined financially and his castle had crumbled. His wife was gone and the children grown up and had fled the nest. So like me he was alone living in this small village where the wind blew so hard each day. He rented a cottage down beyond the hotel by the wood. It had a beautiful view, but the cottage itself was old and in poor repair. I lived across the street from Holland's Bar. My place was old too. I had the upstairs of a house. The sea air had infiltrated it and made it damp and musty, and in the winter the Arctic air filled the rooms like smoke. I made it as cosy as I could, lighting the big open fire from early morning. It was my way of keeping warm.

One morning whilst sitting by my fire I got a text message from Albert; he wanted to see me. Every now and again I got these cryptic invitations, mostly when he wanted something. Most of his text messages were followed by requests like,
"Bring me a bottle of brandy", or "I am out of bread and milk", but this time there was nothing. I was to just come myself. I set off with the wind at my back, walking down the hill by the sea wall. I was thinking that sometimes if you live in a place long enough its beauty grows on you almost to the point that it is painful, as on that morning looking at the trees sweeping down to the tide it sort of got me that way. I watched the swans gliding by and the cormorants wave from the sandbank. The channel was emptying and the gulls knew it, so they screamed at the receding water. On land too autumn had savaged the earth

to allow room for the impending winter. Albert's cottage was up the steep hill. It overlooked the estuary and all in between. When I went in he was sitting by a measly fire, cleaning the frames of his glasses.

'Harry, my good friend, you are early. I was going to make a pot of tea but I am out of fucking teabags, so you can make us both coffee if you have the strength to do it. How are things in North Korea?' he shouted after me.

Looking over my left shoulder I shouted back to him, 'All is well with our society.' I could hear him laugh from the kitchen.

'Nobody starving then?'

I didn't answer as I knew he was just pressing my buttons, and besides I wasn't going to let him drag me into that debate.

'It is cold, but it is dry,' he said when I walked in with two mugs of coffee.

'Hope you didn't put too much milk in mine.'

'I didn't, Al, it is just the way you like it.'

'People are divils for milk, and you end up drinking milk instead of coffee or tea. My mother used to drink coffee black, but that was mainly because we couldn't afford the milk in the first place, you get me?'

'Don't like too much myself; as you say, it fucks it up.'

'I saw the lifeboat go out earlier. Are they on exercise?'

'Dunno, Al,' I said, walking to the window. A small tub of a fishing boat was rounding the channel. It was heading out, so it was light in the water and soon it would pass the green buoy by the wood.

'I am fucked, Harry.'

'Why?'

'I am on the last of my money. It's run out. Those legal bastards have taken the last of it. They fucked me. I was trying to hide a few bob, but they found it, and, sure, you know what happens. I was tryin' to siphon it off to my oldest son, you know, but they blocked it, so now we have nothing, not even the pension. For the first time in my life I am broke, Harry.'

'Jesus. How will you pay the rent?'

'I won't, boy. There is nuthin' there.'

He looked at me for a second, and then he drank his coffee and put on his glasses. His eyes looked bigger behind the lenses.

'Al, I haven't got a cent, I swear. I am cleaned out.'

'Sssh, will you? I don't need a loan, as it would run out in no time. Nah, I have some news for you, my boy.'

'What?'

'I got a job!'

'A job? Where?' '

'A proper job too.'

'Jesus, tell me, will you?'

'Do you know Nina Van Saunders?'

'Never heard of her.'

'Jesus, Harry boy, she is the business around here. Her husband is one of the richest men in the world. He is into everything: stocks and shares and commodities, the markets.' Albert whispered the last part.

'She does loads for charities, and she runs yacht races over in Kinsale. She is the business. Now, like me, she loves a tipple, but we won't hold that against her.'

'Wow. So what's the job then?'

'She knows me from my supermarket days. I used to supply them with stuff for their fetes and put up prizes and all of that. Anyhow, didn't I meet her in Bandon yesterday. We were chatting for ages on the street, but then she said out of the blue, 'Albert boy, come on, and I will stand you a brandy.' I couldn't believe it. She brought me into this bar and stood me three brandies, and she thanked me for all of the service I provided her family over the years. She said that her husband was living in Portugal most of the time, and then she confided that she and Edward were apart now. But to make a long story short, Harry, she wants me to be caretaker of the house out at Dunworley.'

'What about her?'

'They have houses everywhere. I think she said she is staying in Dublin. Now do you credit that?'

'What's the deal?'

'Food and board. You want to see the place. Swimming pool and the view, and she said she would pay me a generous allowance, but I dunno yet. What do you think, Harry, just when I was about to throw myself into the tide, hah?'

'Sounds too good to be true to have a place like that all to yourself. There has to be a catch.' I finished my coffee and went to bring the mug back to the kitchen.

'You had better stoke up that fire, Al, or it will go out. It is to get much colder later.'

'There is a catch, boy. I never told her about losing my licence, so she thinks I can drive. Part of my duties is to collect people from the airport if she has guests come down for the weekend. Like, it might not come up much, as she rarely uses the place, but she says her daughter, Jane, uses it at least once a year, so I dunno. Maybe I should come clean with her and bite the bullet, or maybe not. I could say I am sick or something and you could do the driving, Harry. I might even get you on the payroll, but if not I will fix you up myself.'

'She will hardly buy it, Al. Maybe it would be best to tell her, especially if it won't be that often. Sure, these people can afford taxies, helicopters even.'

'I know, Harry, but the car comes with the place, you know. I have to get supplies in as well. I am afraid this will fuck it up. What do you think?'

'It might, but it might not. What is it; do you not want to have to tell her that they put you off the road?'

149

'No, it doesn't sound good.'
'I know.' He started to stoke the fire and the coals glowed
orange but it was dead looking, so I shovelled a heap of
coal on it and a small rotten log. It worked, as yellow
flames appeared from the rear, but it would be awhile
before it gave out any real heat.
'Tell her, Albert. You have to tell her, but don't say they
put you off the road. Say you have a problem with your
eyes, and the doctor advised you not to drive for six
months. I dunno something like that. It will get you off of
the hook short term, won't it?'
'I really need this job, Harry, otherwise where will I go?
Like, this is it, you know?'

Either he took my advice or he came up with some equally
brilliant plan of his own, but he got the job and he even
managed to get me on the payroll as the driver. They can
say what they like about rich people, but Nina Van
Saunders was very generous and she put me on a retainer of
eight hundred Euros per month and room and board in the
house thrown in. Albert was to look after the food and
drinks, and he was responsible for managing the house and
hiring temporary staff when needed and the sourcing of
suppliers, and also he was just to make sure the place was
kept clean and tidy. I was to drive and look after
maintenance issues with the swimming pool and the
gardens. All in all, as the man said, we were made. The real
bonus however was when Nina Van Saunders said that she
saw the positions as full-time and on-going, which left us
free to leave our respective accommodations. I have to say,
the memories of that first weekend will live with me
forever. Nina Van Saunders was something else. She was
in her early sixties, her hair was dyed blonde, and she still
looked good and fit. She was one of those people who lived

life on the verge of a guffaw, and when Albert introduced me she found me hilarious, or so it seemed.

'Lovely to meet you, Harry, and you are so handsome.' She laughed so much that Albert felt obliged to join her, and then they both stood laughing their heads off before me. I soon learned that she was like that with everything, even when she was giving me instructions about the changing of the pool water. She laughed like the whole thing was one big joke. Soon I found myself laughing along with her as she showed me about the place. The house was huge, set on the headland overlooking the Atlantic Ocean. The driveway wasn't long but it twisted and turned, leading to a gravel area by the imposing front door. The house itself was old, but to the right they had added a car port and to the left a pool house with a decorative swimming pool shaped in a figure of eight. On the Atlantic side they had a terrace and above it a veranda with a cluster of tables and chairs. The pool had a well-stocked bar with beer and stout on draught and an ice machine and a cooler.

'I don't mind you having a few beers, gentlemen,' Nina said, 'but don't go mad on the whiskey, as it is Edward's drink and he covets it. I think he does a stock take every time he is home, as he thinks that I am stealing it.'

'We wouldn't touch it,' Albert said, like he was making himself a solemn promise. When she was finished giving us the guided tour she announced, 'Of course, gentlemen, you do have the full run of the place. All besides Edward's study. He doesn't like anyone going in there. I am not allowed in, so fat chance of anyone else.' I was gobsmacked by the place. There were at least twelve bedrooms, excluding the staff accommodation, and all were en suite. The study that she referred to took up all of the space above the car port and was equivalent in size to three large rooms.

Nina took us to Kinsale for dinner. It was a posh little restaurant overlooking the harbour. She made a toast before and after the meal.

'Best of luck, gentlemen. May this be the start of a beautiful relationship.' She laughed heartily after she said it, so much so that I began to doubt her sincerity, and I wondered whether all of this good fortune was actually a really cruel trick. She drank a whole bottle of wine on her own. Albert had a few brandies, and I stayed on water now that I was the driver. She made the toast again when the meal was finished, and she laughed all over again. The restaurant was plush and the food was good, if a little on the mean side in regards to servings. The wine she drank looked expensive, but she didn't receive a bill. The fat waiter put it on her tab, and I drove us home along the back roads as it was more direct. When we got back Nina brought us to the pool house where she poured me a beer and Albert a brandy. She opened a new bottle of vodka, and she made it with ice and a dash of cola. After one or two drinks her laughing hyena persona changed, and she sat up on a stool between us looking morose. For some inexplicable reason she directed her conversation at me.

'All you see here is money—Edward's money—but his money is no use to me, Harry. No fucking good. We are married thirty-five years and this is all it amounts to, his money and the comfort it brings. I tell you, the man hasn't a civil word for his wife. He keeps company with whores and tramps, and he has such influence that government's bow to him. But at the end of the day I can take or leave all of this. My apartment in Dublin is very modest. I would trade everything you see here, all of it, if I had a man that loved me. Do you believe me, Harry?'

'I do,' I said, unnerved by her candidness.

'Because it is all so fucking useless. If there was a fire it would all burn away, and I often wish for a fire, and I would stand well back and watch it burn.'

I imagined her standing out in the garden in her nightdress, her face illuminated by the roaring fire. I imagined her smiling as it burned. But then she said, 'He has lots of investments. Some of them in armaments, you know. I think they sell the guns to anyone who wants them as long as there is enough money. Edward has no conscience. None. Zilch.' Albert, who had been concentrating on his brandy, went, 'It takes some man to put together a place like this. He must have a lot of talent.'

'Talent? The man has no talent.'

She looked at Albert like he was gone mad.

'He inherited a fortune from his grandmother, and she made it by selling off the lands left to her by her uncle. Money and talent don't always mix, Albert.' Albert smiled at her, unsure of himself. I could sense that he didn't want to contradict her or anger her. She drank a few more vodkas before slipping away quietly to bed. I was being careful as I had to drive her to Kent station the following morning, so I was glad when Albert slipped away also. I made myself tea before hitting the hay, and the following morning I drove Mrs Van Saunders to Cork. She was back in her laughing mode, but she wore sunglasses and I noticed that she had too much pasty makeup on her cheeks. I took the main road to Cork, and she didn't say much but to comment on the weather and the imminent rain.

The next few weeks were good as Albert and I settled into our routines with me doing the physical work and he acting as manager. Over breakfast, which we ate in the kitchen for handiness, he announced that we would need to hold interviews.

'Part-time staff, for when Jane comes for the weekend or Van Saunders arrives unexpectedly himself. We need people who will come at a short notice.'

'Where will you get them?'

'We can put an advert in the West Cork People.
Bet there will be lots of interest, Harry, and imagine us interviewing people for a job. How ironic is that?'

'Tis ironic alright.'

'Pair of thicks.'

'Never. Sure, we are well able. What do we need?'

'Depends on how many come to visit. We need waiters and a decent cook, and I suppose we will need cleaners as well. She said the last lot were useless, so we better get it right. I have to send a list on to her.'

'She is alright, Al.'

'Yeah, she is sound, but you know she is the boss' wife after all, so I wouldn't be getting too familiar. Hee hee, a man with your reputation. She was fine years ago, but she has withered. Women wither, don't they, Harry? Whereas we grow old gracefully.'

'She was fine alright, going on the photographs in the hall. She was a stunner.'

'Yeah, but a fella like Edward Van Saunders, he would get rid of her as soon as she lost her looks. Evidently he gets fashion models and film stars. Why would he want to cuddle up to her? She is past it, even if she is still nice with it. Everything falls neatly into place in their world.'

I agreed with him, and over the next few weeks we interviewed for staff. It was funny, as Albert adopted a rather saintly and knowing approach. He went out of his way not to be condescending or appear brash, but at the same time he was eager to appear knowledgeable and experienced. The waiting staff and the cleaners were easy enough; they were mostly local people just looking for a few extra euros. But the position of cook was harder to fill

154

as an assorted array of oul wans offered their services, and some of them were incredible ugly as well and very rude, which disturbed Albert greatly as he was measuring their affability as much as anything else. We spoke to three different women and a man. He was a trained chef, young and friendly. We were on the brink of offering him the position when he announced that he had no references from his previous position and that he and the proprietor were at loggerheads, and it was more than likely going to end up in the high court.

'Did you ever see such a daft bunch of eejits?' Albert moaned.

'Mad,' I said, 'and some of those women were fearsome. I wouldn't fancy getting a belt of a frying pan from any of them!'

Albert was frustrated.

'Time for a drink and a think, Harry.' And drink he did and this time I joined him and we sat at the bar like two toffs, playing music on the surround sound system. Albert was drinking copious glasses of brandy whilst I raided the fridge for beer. After time I was taken by the soft ripples in the pool, as the water cleansed itself through the state-of-the-art filtration system.

'If only my ex-wife could see me now, Harry,' he said, 'she would die of shock and choke from envy first. She wouldn't believe it!'

'I think Muriel would have her problems too,' I said. 'But Tara would be delighted.'

'Who is Tara?' he asked.

'My daughter, you ignoramus!'

'Jesus, my crew would have the place rifled.'

'They would not.'

'They would for sure.'

'You are joking me.'

'I am half joking. David and Irene are alright, but Danny and Christina are mad altogether. The place would be wrecked. They're as mad as hell, the two of them, with one worse than the other. She spoiled them; they are her youngest.'

'Tara is an angel. Muriel was a good mother. That wasn't why we split up. It was loads of other things, Al, but she was a good mother.'

'Women are fucking mad anyway. Their heads are full of things so trivial. She spoiled the youngest, then gives out continuously about them, and there is no reminding her that she spoiled them and started the whole damn thing in the first place.'

'That's women for you,' I said, but he wasn't listening to me. Then he said, 'I am happy enough now. Yeah, I miss certain things. It is great for a man to have a family, but families move on just like everything else, so nobody's safe, are they? She is hitting the bottle herself now, and the kids are all away doing their own thing, so there would be just the two of us anyway, and me pissing her off and her pissing me off. If she was with me I would always be trying to get away from her and she would always be getting away from me, and I would be the best customer in Holland's Bar and God knows where she would go. It is like we all want to live in this fantasy world, isn't it? Women looking for security and men looking for a bit of how's your father, and we end up bitter because life is not like Hollywood, is it? There is no happy ever after.'

'No, Al, there is not,' I said, getting him another brandy and taking another cool beer for myself.

The next morning I drove him to the village. He wanted to get a few things from the cottage. He had left some clothes and his medical card and some toiletries. When we arrived the village was quiet, and the hollow wind blew down the main street. While he was gone I listened to it as it tossed the trees lining the road, the branches bending forward tight but then released to return to their standing positions. In the distance the wind clapped, as it met with resistance. Twisting and then winding, it cruelly found its way to hassle small boats and make the moorings chime like dropped pot lids. When we arrived back at the Van Saunders' house a fog had descended from the headland above Dunworley, and it rested on the garden, and then through the mist I caught glimpses of the front door, and then Cecilia Hart emerged from somewhere.

'I cun cook ya whatever ya like an I cun clean, bur I don't do toilets ar ironin or anythin' filthy like dat, ya get me, Al? Big Al, de kiddies' pal!' She was twenty-four years old, but she looked about nineteen. She had short blonde hair tucked up under a black beret. She was of average height but she took to hunching, which took inches from her. When she stood upright her body slimmed down, but if she hunched her tummy rounded like she had a series of marbles attached to a belt.

'I need a place to crash, so if ya's want ya cun deduct it from mi pay. Dats if ya's want, Al. Are ya the boss? But tell us who de real boss is. Yer too nice to be de man. Is de boss a man?' When she removed the beret, her hair fell to the base of her neck and I had been fooled as it was longer than I thought. Then I was smitten, as she had light blue eyes laced with gems, and somehow I wanted to touch and caress her soft pale skin.

'Wat do ya do?'

'I drive and fix things,' I said.

'Wher ar yah from? Not round here.'

'Dublin.'

'Dublin. Yer havin' a laugh. Yer not a Dub. If ya ar yer a fuckin' posh bollix.'

'I am.'

'Wat, a posh bollix or a Dub?'

'A Dub, born and bred.'

'Wit a silver spoon, I'd say.'

'No, the opposite.'

'Yeah, I fuckin' believe ya; thousands wudn't.'

'Where are you from?'

'If I told ya I'd 've to kill yah.'

Then Albert goes, 'I will have to ask Mrs Van Saunders, but there is loads of room. I will check it with her.'

'Alright, Al. Tell her I don't need money, just pocket money. Dat's if she gives mi a room. Bet she's a dry oul wan. I fucking hate dry oul wans. Is she a dry ould cunt?'

'She is alright. She likes a drink,' I said. Cecilia smiled at me like she was happy to concede on this point of vulgarity, but somehow she gave me the impression that there was much more to come.

In the months that followed I somehow lost confidence in my perception of all that was going on around me, and it is fair to say that Cecilia's presence unsettled me greatly. When I look back on the events, I have great difficulty placing them in the correct chronological order as they occurred. Rather, I remember snippets of conversation and many silences that perhaps may have given clues as to what was about to happen. But I do not judge and condemn myself entirely, as there was no way of knowing in advance. In truth only the gods could have known. I had sex with Cecilia many times but only in my own head. Perhaps it was better to have it there than nowhere, and Albert didn't have sex with her either although I know she raised old fires within him. I know she preferred him over me. However she teased us relentlessly, not only with the things she said but also in the way she took to sitting at the pool bar at night in her dressing gown, her bare legs draping to below the bottom rung of her stool. She allowed us endless views of her thighs, and to be honest it was maddening. I was wishing that she didn't do it at all for after I consumed a few beers I would turn my attention to her steel lips, lured by the aroma of dark perfume that was attacking my nostrils. She talked endlessly; shutting us both up for the most part, and Albert was very patient with her whereas I would want to interject when she said outrageous things.

'Dey tuck over de country, Al,' she said.

'I'm not fuckin' jokin' ya, Al boy, dat's wat dey did, sided wit de Brits, den wat? Fuckin' mayhem. Dey fuckin' murdered all de lefties so dey had de state to demselves!' She took a sup of her beer then gargled it as she swallowed. 'Fuckin' lovely, dis beer. Lovely ice cold. Harry, fair fuckin' play far stockin' it up.

'We had a professor in college, before dey fucked me out, like. He cum up wit it. He called de civil war a coup d' état. De rich an de Brits,1922, is wat he said. Now dis fella was a dirty bollix, bur he was a smart dirty bollix, so after dat I joined de rah. Den dey fucked me out, 'cause I was too mad, ta violent dey said. Imagine dat, Harry, gettin' fucked out of de rah far bein' violent, huh. But dey did, an I wus pissed off big time. So dats wen I had mi breakdown. I wus fucked, lads. Dey wer talkin' bout sociopaths an sycophants. Den dey said I was a schizophrenic. Mad or wat?'

'Never heard of it like that,' Albert said.

'Like, we had a civil war alright, but a coup d' état, never read that. Sure, didn't the country vote in 1922? The people had their say.'

'Dey fuckin' rigged dat, Al. Sure, loads people didn't vote at all. Loads of wimman, sure, dey wer anti-treaty. Most of tem anyhow.'

'Never heard it,' Albert reiterated.

'Me neither,' I said.

159

'Yah look it up on de net. Prof Byrdon. He said it, de dirty baldy fecker, bur he said it an wrote a paper on it, so fuck yahs. Suppose ya's cun hardly read anyway, stupid fuckers, yahs.' When she had more beer the legs would show but the rant would continue until the early hours, and Albert confided to me that he was tempted to let her go. However she turned out to be a very capable cook and they were thin on the ground so Albert compromised, deciding that she would be confined to the kitchen when guests arrived. One day I was doing stuff in the pool room, and she came in for a swim. It was early evening, and she had been working hard in the kitchen and cleaning around the house all day. I didn't want to look, but I had to as she strolled to the ladder. I could see she had a great body with milky skin, yet the top of her shoulders were tanned. I noticed her thighs were bigger than the rest of her and that her bottom was long rather than rounded, which I liked. Somehow I sensed that she knew I was watching, and then she did something extraordinary. She undid the bra of her bikini and then dropped her pants so I could see the full length of her bottom, and then she turned and I had to show myself from behind the bar. She smiled at me, and for a second I froze wondering how she wanted me to react but she just turned and dived into the pool and she stayed under water for at least two minutes. So long in fact that I became worried. I went quickly to the edge of the pool but then she surfaced gracefully and lay on her back and I could see her privates, so I turned away save for she might think me a kind of a pervert.

Later she was having a beer and she said to me, 'Wher's yer wife, Harry, is she dead?'
'Nah, she is in Dublin.'
'Da ya have kids?'
'A daughter.'

'Wat fuckin' age is she?'

'She is grown up.'

'Da you miss her?'

'Sometimes.'

'Da ya miss yer missus?'

'Not anymore. Not now.'

'Why?'

'Just don't. It has been a long time.'

'Ya must have loved her once. Ya did, ya pillock!'

'Maybe.'

'Fuck off. Ye were married. Ya had a child!'

'I know, but things change. Nothing stays the same. We grew apart.'

'Bet ya fucked up yer child's head, silly bollix.'

'Hope not.'

'Hope not? Listen to ya, takin' crap. Ya know ya did. Ya left de little girl alone, ya fuckin' sap. Dah ya tink dats alright? She won't suffer ar be hurt?'

'Lots of kids are hurt, Cecilia, but so are adults. You leave people because kids are being hurt in the hope that it will stop so they can deal with life and they can be strong.'

'Mi Da left me Ma. He went ta England wit a slut. Me ma said dat he was ridin' her far years. Den he took a figary an fucked off wit her. Left me an me sister, fucker. Ya see de hurt now, Harry?'

Albert had stayed quiet up to now, but he went,

'Can't judge, Cecilia. Life isn't perfect and I was king of the castle, but when the castle fell down my wife left me, and the kids all bogged off too. Kings are only as good as their hordes of gold.'

'Big Al, talkin' like a fuckin' poet. Ya know, dey said dat was wat drove me fuckin' mad—de abandonment. Dat an Professor Byrdon's paper on de fuckin' coup d' état, 'cause I got pissed bout de fuckers sidin' wit de Brits an de church, den robbin' our country.'

'Ah, Jesus, she is on about all that nonsense again, Harry,'
Albert said wearily, but she just laughed and said, 'Ta fuck
if ya don't get it. How de fuck did de bourgeoisie get to run
dis little island wit only five million on it? Der has only
been emigration an poverty, nuthin' else. Dey run de show.
Everywhere ya go, dey ar fuckin' wit de place, privatisin'
everytin' an cuttin services an robbin' de poor citizen.'
'Wat will ya two pillocks do bout it? If ya get sick, ya have
to pay. Den de toffs have der private medicine wher dey
tink it's ok to have an operation in de 'private hospital.'
'Oh my lord, Albert, an lord, Harry, de fuckin' private
hospital. Like, wat happened to de fuckin' state an de
public system? Fuckers ar tearin' it apart so poor fuckers
have to pay. Dats wats happenin', ya silly cunts.'
'Hah, they try all of this in North Korea. Is that want you
want, girl? The world to be in black and white, where we
share everything and everyone ends up starved?'
Albert went red in the face, and in reaction Cecilia pulled
her night gown below her knee. He helped himself to
another brandy whilst she gargled another beer. Then I
said, 'North Korea is not an example of an equitable
society, to be honest, Al. It doesn't wash. Society can be
fair and equitable and still productive. Social conscience, I
think it is called.'
'Fuckin' social conscience, is dat it? Yer fuckin' mad,
Harry. At least big Al is straight up, like he doesn't hide dat
he's an asshole. But ya do like a fuckin' rat. Social
conscience? Wat da fuck is dat? Dis country was stolen by
capitalism. Dey used guns an bombs. If ya tink wer gonna
get it back without guns an bombs, yer fuckin' mad. Social
conscience ta fuck!'

By day Cecilia worked feverishly, and in the evening she
would swim naked in the pool always performing the same
routine, I guess, whether we were there or not. Sometimes

162

Albert and I might be drinking at the bar, but it didn't
bother her nor in the end did it bother us, as we had just got
used to it and to her. She took to patrolling the house,
keeping all of the rooms spick and span, airing the bed
linen, and hoovering up the dust. Albert rang Nina Van
Saunders to update her, and he expressly praised Cecilia
and Mrs Van Saunders laughed when Albert mentioned
revolution. She advised him that Edward was coming home
for a week at the end of the month, and he had invited his
daughter, Jane, to join him, along with some friends and a
politician he knew. She laughed again, telling Albert to
expect a minister and armed guards. Albert was in great
form the rest of the day, as the thought of guests excited
him. It was time to put his great plan into place and to get
in touch with the entire staff and book them in for that
week. He spent the whole afternoon stocktaking whilst I
cleaned the car and Cecilia washed pillow cases and guest
towels. When we met that evening she was dressed in jeans
and a dark jumper. She hadn't visited the pool as normal so
I guessed that she was cold, but she told me she wasn't.
'I don't always lie around in mi dressing gown. Wishful
thinkin', Harry boy. Nah, I was gonna ask yah for a lift to
de village, but I changed mi mind now. Why ya fuckin'
care beats me anyhow, bur yer an asshole so maybe dats
why.'
Albert, sensing an opportunity, said, 'We better behave
when the minster comes. I hear Edward Van Saunders is
very tough, so we best lay low when he is here. Cecilia,
like, no messing, girl. You know, he says jump, we say
how high.' I nodded in support but Cecilia, looking at me,
said, 'Fuck him an his ministers. Wat ar dey minsters of,
Al? Dis aint a proper state. Dey stole it back in '22, so da
fuck wit 'em!'
'Don't mess this up, girl,' Albert said.

'Harry and I need this job. If you are not happy, well, you know what you can do, but we need this job because we have nothing else.'

'Big Al is gettin' pissed off, Harry. He tinks I'm goin to fuck it up far him. Ah, Albert, I won't. I spent three months in a locked ward once. Da ya tink I wanna go back der?'

'Three months?' I said.

'They should have kept it locked,' Albert said but I could see he was sorry that he said it, and she blushed but she didn't make a smart answer.

She just said, 'De worst ting ever wus dem turnin' de key every night. I hated dat sound.'

The following afternoon Albert suggested we go for a walk. It was his way of making up to her. It came as a relief, as we all had been flat out preparing for our visitors. We walked down the steep hill and then onto the road that led to the beach at Dunworley. Cecilia was taken with the rock formations. She got lost amongst them and disappeared into the caverns whilst Albert and I walked by the shoreline. We eventually settled, leaning against an outcrop of purple rock.

'We have it made, Harry boy,' he said, the wind tossing his white hair, which disturbed his normal settled appearance. 'There was you giving up hope, banging the communist drum, but in sails good old capitalism to save the day. May God bless Nina Van Saunders.'

I laughed as I wanted to tell him that I didn't feel in the least bit made and that I had more ambition than to see myself as the driver for some millionaire for the rest of my days, but I didn't. I just said, 'It is sound alright.' Cecilia ran over to us excitedly, 'De water is so fuckin' clear. Jesus, I never seen anythin' like it.' Albert moved over to allow her to rest against the rock.

'Fuckin' crazy rocks. Luk at de colours. Mad blues an purples. Beaut country, Ireland, worth fightin' for, Al.' Albert, ignoring her, walked to the waters edge, avoiding the wash that seemed to react to his presence by coming in stronger and almost wetting his shoes.

'He wus sayin' he was rich. Is he spoofin' us?' Cecilia asked me.

'Nah, he owned three supermarkets before the recession hit.'

'Dah yah wanna be rich, Harry?'

'Dunno. Maybe. Wouldn't mind having a few bob.'

'How can ya be rich an still be a socialist den?'

'Socialism is about the division of profit, not about personal wealth. I could never change my mind on that.'

'Yer a great fella wit a social conscience. Tell mi, Harry, how cum it's alrite far rich people to kill poor people from afar, like tru wars an stuff, but wen poor people fight back its terrorism, like?' She reached into her pocket and produced her beret. When she put it on she looked like a female Che Guevara. Then she ran to where Albert was standing and ran around him in circles till he tired of her and he came back to me.

'The girl is bonkers, but who cares on such a beautiful day?'

She was quiet for a time that night, and she was fully dressed for a change. Albert suggested that we should all take it easy; as the first guests were due to arrive tomorrow. He supped a brandy, and Cecilia and I just had beers.

'It is a great break for me. This I never dreamed of,' he said, looking around him, admiring the pool and the beautiful furniture.

'It is the life, my friend. I took you out of the slums to bring you here.'

I didn't comment, as I wasn't sure if he was just bein'
warm and friendly or was there some subliminal message
underneath it all.

'How did ya lose de supermarkets?' Cecilia asked out of
the blue.

'Like de fuckers still shop, no matter wat. Recession mi
arse.'

Albert looked directly at her for a moment I thought he was
about to explode, but he didn't. He just said quietly,
'Because I bought a lot of property that lost its value, that's
why.' Cecilia winked at me but Albert could well see her,
and she countered with, 'Bollix, ya see, 'cause every
muther fucker wants property. Isn't dat wat it's all about?
Fuckin' property, so all men ar kings in der own state. Sure,
dats why der is such poverty, 'cause fuckers like yah Al,
wanna own everytin'.' Albert sighed; he looked at me,
exasperated, but before he could speak she said, 'De state
owns de land, not you. Der, you see, de state can lease it to
ya, but ya don't own nuthin'. De country belongs to de
citizens, see.'

'I would hardly go that far,' I said seriously.

'Nah, ya wuldn't, yer social conscience wud be offended.
But if nobody owned property, tink of it, how equal wud
tings be?'

'We're back in North Korea where they starve!' Albert
shouted.

'In capitalism half de world starves!'

'Tell her,' Albert instructed me.

'You're saying nobody should own property?'

'De state owns everytin'. Wer born to de state. It minds an
cares far us, from cradle ta de fuckin' grave. Don't ya see,
dats why dey shot de boys in 1922, to fuckin' stop dis
happenin'!'

'Christ, heard it all. Now what? She would have us all
runnin' around in grey suits. Hah hee hee!'

'Big Al tinks he is not runnin' around. Dats all ya do, ya daft fucker!'

Albert went to help himself to another brandy, but I had enough and I was ready to retire. Yet I didn't want to leave her, as suddenly it became like watching the television with the sound down. She spoke so rapidly using expletives, but I was staring at her perfect skin and her bone structure that was made of marble stone. She infected me with her eyes, and when glancing at me she aroused my senses in a way that was new and unique. Every so often Albert would snarl back at her, but it just made her solidify until her beauty enraptured me, and the words she used spun around in my brain.

'So ya have all dese mad fuckers runnin' tru shopping malls. Retail, Al, everytin' is retail. De fuckin' world is retail. Sell me somethin', Al. Cum on, Al. Here, I'll sell ya mi body. Ya two can do me for a fifty. How bout it, Al?'

She stood and started to undress, and Albert watched her remove her top and then undo her bra. He kept telling her to stop, but she kept on going until I stood up and shouted angrily, 'Put your clothes back on! Who do you think we are?' She stopped undressing, looking at me coldly.

'Yer men wit a big hard on. Do ya tink I doubt it? De two of ya like spinsters. Lost ta de world. Al here deep down loves da system. Harry wit da social conscience. Yis ar full of shit!'

And she left and went to bed, and Albert had one more drink to settle himself and I went to bed but I couldn't sleep a wink.

The following morning, I went to the kitchen to see if Cecilia wanted more supplies for the dinner party but she wasn't there so I went around the house looking for her. After an age I eventually found her in the extension over the car port. She was rummaging in the forbidden Edward

Van Saunders study. I didn't want to make a big deal of it as she had a mop and bucket and a duster with her, so I presumed she was just cleaning with enthusiasm. She smiled at me as she locked the door with a set of keys that she had found someplace. It turned out that she had all she needed save for some self-raising flour, carrots, onions, and some cucumber. That evening I went to the airport to collect Jane Van Saunders and three of her friends, two men and a woman. The men were quiet if reserved but the woman was a pain in the arse, all the way back talking relentlessly about property investments and how her father had left her too much money. Jane was a slight thing with a tiny face and a pointed nose. She was doll-like with waxed skin, and she wasn't very tall. Her hair was cropped short, and though she wore casual clothes they reeked of expensive designer labels. The men went to their rooms to prepare for their pre-dinner drinks. Albert was doing barman whilst the waiting staff assisted in the kitchen. I found it hard to get used to the sight of strangers in our pool room, drinking in what I suddenly began to view as our bar. When they all gathered the men wore dress suits and the women were in evening dress, and I got a sudden urge to ask them all to leave. Albert escorted the party upstairs to the dining room, and the waiters attended with poise and by all accounts the food was excellent, and compliments were extended gracefully to the chef. I didn't see Cecilia as she did as requested and stayed in her kitchen. The guests all retired back to the poolside bar, and Albert attended to them again. This time one of the male guests was a little drunk, and he made inappropriate advances on the pain-in-the-arse woman. She seemed to enjoy it at first but then she became aggravated, and Jane Van Saunders spoke to the man sternly. He waved his arms at her cheekily, and Albert took his drink away and replaced it with water. Eventually they all left and went to their respective beds and Albert and I had a drink, but Cecilia was tired and she went to bed.

The guest party wanted to go touring the next day, so I drove them back to the surf beach at Dunworley and then around the headland to Ballinglanna and on to Ring and Clonakilty where they did some shopping. The drunken man of the night before was particularly quiet, and it was obvious that the pain-in-the-arse woman still wasn't speaking to him and that Jane Van Saunders was also short with him but not quite at the not-speaking level. When they got back they repeated the routine of the previous day but they skipped the pool bar after the meal, sitting on drinking wine at the dinner table. I was pleased that our little bar didn't have to suffer them, and Albert said afterwards that all they discussed were matters of high finance and the tragic marriage breakups of their friends.

The following morning Edward Van Saunders arrived. He was very small in stature with grey hair above his ears, but he was bald on top. He wore an expensive suit, but somehow I thought that his shoes were grubby and a little out of place with the rest of his attire. He was accompanied by a blonde woman in her early thirties. She was very elegant with lots of makeup, and he introduced her as his personal assistant, Ms Spencer. I wondered just how she assisted him but then reasoned that it was none of my shagging business, and fair play to the man. After all he was getting on himself. I found Edward Van Saunders cold, but I have to also say that he was very polite and mannerly. He asked me about the new staff and arrangements at Dunworley, and when I explained all to him he seemed satisfied with his wife's endeavours. Back in the house he took charge and he asked Albert to summon all of the staff to the pool house, as he wanted to meet them individually and he did, shaking hands with each in turn as Albert introduced them. He stopped at Cecilia and smiled. I could tell he was sizing her up. She held her hand out weakly and he held it, but not for long as she withdrew it smartly. He held his gaze for a second before moving on to the waiters. He told Albert that the minister of defence would be arriving later with his entourage and that we were to provide him with every courtesy. Albert got very excited, as he was a real fan of Jim Bowen for many years and indeed had voted for him in the Cork East constituency when he had lived there. The thoughts of meeting the minister face to face pleased him greatly.

The afternoon was a busy one with the food preparation and the seating arrangements. Evidently the minister and Edward Van Saunders were to retire to the study before the meal, and a bottle of whiskey and brandy were to be delivered when Edward Van Saunders opened the study. The minister duly arrived with his entourage, including his private secretary and two plain clothes Garda who wore tight-fitting suits. They patrolled the perimeter of the house as the minister was escorted through the hallway to shake hands with Edward Van Saunders who arrived smartly down the stairs. Minister Bowen was a big portly man with a fat face. He was bright red on the cheeks, and he had big brown eyes and greying hair that had been dyed to look blonde. He was dressed in his ministerial suit and his private secretary, a little man with glasses, trailed after him like he was been dragged on a lead. They had their whiskey and brandy delivered, and altogether they spent forty-five minutes in the study. Then they emerged with loud laughter and with lots of back slapping to be greeted by the waiting Miss Spencer who had been excluded from the meeting. The minister was thoroughly enjoying himself as he entered the pool bar to greet the other guests who all stood and clapped. He was introduced to all of the guests by Edward Van Saunders, and Albert was busy making drinks behind the bar. I went to his aid so as not to delay them. The minister and the entourage all sat by the pool. He was drinking whiskey along with Edward Van Saunders who now had Miss Spencer alongside.

When Cecilia came in I noticed the smoke bellowing down the hall behind her. She was dressed like she was ready to go outside. She wore her black beret and a leather jacket. Nobody took any notice of her at first until she screamed, 'Dis is far all de boys ya murdered in yer coup d' état!' The minister was on his feet and Edward Van Saunders did likewise. He had his back to her, so he had to turn around. Then I saw that she had a handgun, and she pointed it directly at the minister. Jane Van Saunders screamed, and her pain-in-the-arse friend wailed. The young men stood watching helplessly.
'Dis is far dem!'
She shot the minister through his forehead, and he collapsed immediately. Edward Van Saunders shouted something about his gun. Then he said clearly, 'She has my gun!'
The minister's private secretary was desperately trying to save his boss. Miss Spencer covered her face with her hands; she was too frightened to scream. Albert, who was stunned, raised enough energy to shout, 'No, Cecilia, no!' She shot Edward Van Saunders right through the head; he fell to the ground, blood gushing on to the floor as he fell. It made dark purple pools.
'See, Harry, dis is easy!' Cecilia shouted.
What happened next is still a blur. I think the two Garda bodyguards arrived and opened fire on her. She returned fire and injured both but she fell, and when Albert went to her side one of the injured detectives shot him right through

his left ear. The smoke had consumed the whole house by now, but somehow I dragged both Cecilia's and then Albert's body out into the garden. I watched over them, the blood sapping through my hands red and sticky as I laid them out side by side, around me screams of terror as the men tried to carry the other bodies outside, and Jane Van Saunders still screaming watched the flames burn. But the pain-in-the-arse woman just stood dumb, staring helplessly at her.

When I returned to the village the wind had ceased, and a black cat spat at me from a distance. Randomers ran for cover as I approached, each one scowling before disappearing down drains, and as I walked up the main street the wind lifted once more but this time more piercing and desperate than ever. It rustled through the festival bunting before cutting through the exposed buildings like a knife, all black handled and shiny 'til I heard the demolition, the convoluted story, the truth, brought with it the sea and history. Then me, on my knees, saw all of those idealists die right in front of me for the want of not making sense. Then the wind gave us paper with numbers on it and the drains opened and the cats groaned, and the manholes closed. Slither, slither. Children saw the pot of gold at the end of this almighty road.

'I still hold that our right to be regarded as the legitimate government of this country is faulty, that this house itself is faulty. You have secured the de facto position. Very well. There must be somebody in charge to keep order in the community, and by virtue of your de facto position you are the only people who are in a position to do it. But as to whether you have come to that position legitimately or not, I say you have not come to that position legitimately. You brought off a coup d' état in the summer of 1922.'

Eamonn de Valera- Dail Eireann

ABOUT THIS AUTHOR

Paul Kestell was born in Sallynoggin, Dublin in 1958. He has published two novels and two books of novelettes. He also had a play broadcast on RTE radio.

9475163R00101

Printed in Great Britain
by Amazon.co.uk, Ltd.,
Marston Gate.